I'LL BE RIGHT BACK

OTHER BOOKS BY TOM WAYMAN

Poetry:
Waiting For Wayman, 1973
For and Against the Moon: Blues, Yells, and Chuckles, 1974
Money and Rain: Tom Wayman Live!, 1975
Free Time: Industrial Poems, 1977
A Planet Mostly Sea, 1979
Living on the Ground: Tom Wayman Country, 1980
Introducing Tom Wayman, 1980
The Nobel Prize Acceptance Speech, 1981
Counting the Hours: City Poems, 1983
The Face of Jack Munro, 1986
In a Small House on the Outskirts of Heaven, 1989
Did I Miss Anything?, 1993
The Astonishing Weight of the Dead, 1994

Essays:
Inside Job: Essays on the New Work Writing, 1983
A Country Not Considered: Canada, Culture, Work, 1993

Editor:
Beaton Abbot's Got the Contract, 1974
A Government Job at Last, 1976
Going for Coffee, 1981
East of Main (with Calvin Wharton), 1989
Paperwork, 1991

I'LL BE RIGHT BACK

New and Selected Poems 1980–1996

TOM WAYMAN

Ontario Review Press · Princeton

The Ontario Review Press
9 Honey Brook Drive
Princeton, New Jersey 08540

Distributed by George Braziller, Inc.
171 Madison Avenue
New York, New York 10016

Library of Congress Cataloging-in-Publication Data

Wayman, Tom, 1945–
I'll be right back : new and selected poems,
1980–1996 / Tom Wayman
I. Title
PR9199.3.W39148 1997 811'.54—dc20 96-44949
ISBN 0-86538-086-4 (pbk.)

Cover: photo by Jeremy Addington

First Edition

ACKNOWLEDGMENTS

I wish to particularly thank the editors of Ontario Review Press, Raymond Smith and Joyce Carol Oates, for their ongoing support, encouragement and hospitality to my words. To have received such generosity is one of the greatest pleasures of my writing life.

I am grateful as well to the editors of the periodicals and anthologies in whose pages these poems first appeared. And I am deeply appreciative of the publishers and their staffs who issued the collections from which the present selection is made: McClelland and Stewart, Harbour Publishing, and Polestar Press. I owe a special debt to Howard White of Harbour Publishing for years of friendship and inspiration, and to Michelle Benjamin of Polestar Press for her imagination and assistance. Thanks, too, to the Master of Massey College at the University of Toronto, John Fraser, and all the Massey College community for their innumerable kindnesses to me during Spring Term 1996 while I was compiling this book.

Poems here are selected from the following volumes: *Counting the Hours* (McClelland and Stewart, 1983), *The Face of Jack Munro* (Harbour, 1986), *In a Small House on the Outskirts of Heaven* (Harbour, 1989), *Did I Miss Anything? Selected Poems 1973–1993* (Harbour, 1993) and *The Astonishing Weight of the Dead* (Polestar, 1994). All but *Counting the Hours* are still in print. My sincere thanks to Harbour Publishing and to Polestar Press for permission to reprint.

The Introduction to *I'll Be Right Back* first appeared in a longer form in *Did I Miss Anything?* Previously uncollected poems here were published in *Caliban, Canadian Forum, Event, Malahat Review, Ontario Review*.

I dedicate this book to the memory of my mother, Sara Zadkin Wayman, 1910–1995.

CONTENTS

from THE ASTONISHING WEIGHT OF THE DEAD (1994)

NEW POEMS

INTRODUCTION: WHAT WORK DOES

The past two decades and more have been a wonderful experience for me as a writer, and for my poems. In 1973 my first collection, *Waiting For Wayman*, was published in Canada, and in 1980 Ontario Review Press honored my first seven years of book publication by issuing a selected poems to that date, *Introducing Tom Wayman*. The present volume, *I'll Be Right Back*, offers what I consider to be the most memorable poems I have published since 1980. Also here are some new poems that bring the reader up to the present.

In the years since 1973 my words and I have had more than our share of recognition, media attention, public readings, literary festivals, magazine and anthology publication, grants, translations into other languages, awards, writer-in-residenceships...everything, in fact, that any author could want. Meanwhile, I have watched helplessly as the art form I love has diminished in the public's perception of its value and importance. Arrayed against poetry is a swelling and seemingly unbeatable coalition that includes a declining readership for any written material, the adoption of poetry as an instrument of torture in our secondary school classrooms, and the confusion by a number of authors between obscurity of presentation and depth of thought, and between exclusiveness and superiority.

However, like a steadily-promoted deck officer on the *Titanic*, I have been having a marvellous time as a writer. During the past decades my poems have taken me to fascinating places, and introduced me to many amazing and delightful people, that otherwise I never would have known. I also have been privileged to help bring into being—along with dozens of others—a new movement in poetry, literature, and the arts generally: the incorporation into the human story of the actual conditions and effects of daily employment. In this task my contribution has been the editing of anthologies and the writing of essays, in addition to my own poems. The endeavor, however, has introduced me and my poetry to non-literary audiences that the already-blazed cultural trails would never have led me to. These audiences, along with the first-year college classes I teach, have provided me with a continual reminder of the ever-widening gap between literary pursuits and the concerns of a majority of my fellow citizens.

Yet throughout these years, my poetic aim has been to provide an accurate depiction of our common everyday life. I have tried to combine this with a sense of humor and with a vision of a better possibility for people than what we have so far achieved. My hope is that the latter two aspects of my writing provide perspective on the balance of what I portray. As for spirituality, I long ago was a convert to the concept expressed by Robert Bly in his poem "Turning Away from Lies" (from *The Light Around the Body*, 1967): "The Kingdom of Heaven does not mean the next life / ... The two worlds are both in this world."

Overall, my intention is that the complexities revealed by my poems should be the complications of our everyday existence, rather than newly-created difficulties or mysteries generated by tricks of language or poetic form. Clarity, honesty, accuracy of statement have been my goals—subject to, naturally, the limits of human discourse found in *every* genre or means of communication. My aim is that my poems should be useful: to myself, and to others who share my community and world. I mean these poems to be a gift; I want my poetry to be a tender, humorous, enraged, piercing, but always accurate depiction of where we are—as individuals functioning in a society, and as members of a rawly self-conscious species now occupying the third planet from a nondescript star.

Much that I have encountered in my life in the way of events, individuals, and popular and high art has influenced my writing. In poetry, two important Canadian influences were Earle Birney and Al Purdy. I was impressed by the range of their subject matter and by their careful craftsmanship, even though the latter often appears within a deceptively conversational tone. Internationally, my major influences were T. S. Eliot and, in translation, Pablo Neruda. I attended university at a time when Eliot dominated English letters. For many years the shadow of Eliot lay across whatever I wrote; my "Asphalt Hours, Asphalt Air" is an attempt to banish that dry darkness forever. The poem is based closely on Eliot's *The Waste Land*, but my poem places its concerns within a landscape of contemporary North American myths and activities. Neruda has been a much sunnier and more vigorous model for me. The Chilean poet's attention to the real elements of this world—things—and his huge affection for people have influenced many poems of mine, including "New and Used," where the initial inspiration came from Neruda's poem about a Valparaiso clockmaker.

What I bring to poetry that these writers do not is the centrality of daily work to our life. I believe that to try to articulate the human story without depicting the core of daily existence is a tragic mistake. We all dream of a world without work, but we remain victims of our form of social organization as long as we—and our art—refuse to honestly consider how our jobs shape us, positively and negatively.

Because many of us do not like what we see when we look at our jobs, we frequently engage as individuals and a community in acts of denial about daily employment. Most jobs constitute a distinct society we participate in each day, where during this central part of our existence most of the democratic rights and privileges North Americans enjoy off the job are suspended. Briefly, we live our productive lives—the majority of our waking hours—as free-lance serfs. We are free to chose and change the masters we will obey for money, free to be destitute or marginal, free to go into debt, free to purchase as many of life's necessities and/or drugs and toys as our rate of remuneration permits. We are even free to employ other serfs. But most of us at work have no significant control over what happens to us, over who gives us orders, over the organization of production, over the distribution of the wealth our labor produces, over the social uses of what we create. The alternative of self-employment often turns into self-exploitation as we strive to compete with enterprises employing serfs.

The majority of our society's artifacts—educational, cultural, commerical—turn a blind eye to the conditions of our employment and to how our occupations function as a governing influence on our existence. Yet every human emotion is part of work. Joy, wonder, laughter, unhappiness, rebellion, lust, love can be experienced at the jobsite, since work—however undemocratically structured today—is in its last analysis a place where human beings gather to remanufacture the world. Every activity found in the shop or office or factory, however, is warped by its occurrence within a more-or-less authoritarian environment, just as our lives are warped by our and our neighbors' daily participation in this environment. We deny this, as a society, at our peril. I do not see my role as a literary artist as contributing—through denial—to the ongoing affliction of myself or my friends and co-workers.

As an author, I owe much to many people who have helped me and my poems; some of these are listed on the Acknowledgments page here. But the main portion of my gratitude must go to my readers, who despite the prevailing aesthetic have welcomed not only my poems but also the vision of literature toward which I struggle. It is ultimately my readers' response that has made my artistic adventures during these decades such intensely rewarding ones. How can I express an overwhelming gratitude? Near the end of Marcel Camus' 1958 film *Orfeu Negro* (*Black Orpheus*), the grieving Orpheus asks this same question of his beloved Euridice, whose dead body he is carrying in his arms. She has given him total happiness, has immeasurably enriched his life; how can he tell her this? His friend Hermes, who like Orpheus in Camus' version of the myth is a Rio de Janeiro transit company employee, advises: "Say a poor man's word, Orpheus: 'thank you.'"

To all my readers, then—past, present and future—I say: *thank you.*

from
COUNTING THE HOURS:
CITY POEMS
(1983)

WATCHING A YOUNG WOMAN KILL HERSELF

As we drove up the long span
of the suspension bridge,
just before where the deck
reaches the first of the two high towers,
the car in front of us stopped
in its lane, and a young woman
got out, closed the door
and ran toward the edge
and without pausing
leaped to clear the four-foot iron railing
and was gone:
                    No,
as we passed her car, jamming on our brakes
we saw her hands
had caught the outside of the rail
behind her as she jumped, so she hung there
—her fingers pointing toward us. And Don
was out of the driver's seat and running
back down the bridge toward her, and me
opening the car door so slowly
not wanting this to be happening
wanting to be somewhere else
so I was only at the back of the car
when Don was five feet away from her
when her hands vanished

at 6:15 in the afternoon.

                              Ambassador Bridge
                              Windsor-Detroit
                              28 April 1976

ASPHALT HOURS, ASPHALT AIR

for Ron Baxter and Bron Wallace

*Men are as mature
as the forces of production
of their times allow them to be.*
—T.W. Adorno

1 *Quitting in the Spring*

Windsor, eight a.m.; the shifts already begun.
In the light rain, a man eating breakfast in his car
on the Kentucky Fried Chicken lot: the revolving sign
broken, fluorescent tubes
visible through the missing plastic.

Curbside trees
keep some of the sidewalk dry.
Groups of children are headed for school
carrying books and umbrellas.
A girl driving a small car
stops for another girl
who gets in, smiling.

> "At the plant, this guy in his late fifties
> has a bench alongside the tool crib
> for his chests of spare parts: the repairman.
> If something is broken on a drill
> or a fitting gone on an air hose,
> we usually say, 'Throw it out.' But he
> will carefully manufacture small copper washers
> to fix the routers, and take all morning
> to loosen a hand jigsaw we can't get to budge.
> Inside the lid of one of his chests
> is a row of ticket stubs
> to the Union's Christmas party
> for the past sixteen years. In the midst of all the bustle,
> somehow he has gotten a corner
> to work away at things at his own pace."

"When I went back after a year
the foreman says—he was taking me around
in a bunch of new-hires—he says to me:
'We'll put you over here, son, to start.
It's not too difficult.'
'That's good,' I told him,
'because I'm *real* dumb,
and I work *real* slow.'
He looked at me for a second:
'You've worked here before,' he says."

      "Once I decide I'm going to quit
      it's like doing hard time in jail:
      I know I shouldn't
      but I count down.
      The last job I had, warehousing,
      I was going to quit in the Spring
      but then decided to stay on through August
      and finally gave my notice
      for the end of September.
      I guess everybody does it a little—
      some guys always have it figured
      how many weeks until their vacations,
      and the crew by the small parts spray booth
      put up a sign each December:
      'Only 14 working days until Christmas.'
      But with me, once I know I'm going
      I can tell you how many more *minutes*
      I have left to work."

In the small grocery store on Wyandotte
after school hours or on weekends
the son or daughter are at the cash register:
both in their teens, bored and sullen,
throwing the customers' purchases into the bags,
while their grandfather
sits on a soft drink crate behind them
reading his newspaper.

"Occasionally when it rains
I'll be up at Final Assembly fixing parts short
and I feel the cold air
coming in despite the heaters.
I look through the doors,
and for a few minutes
I'm happy to be inside, working."

"Somebody stuck an announcement
on the Union bulletin board
attacking the executive for calling a second vote
on the dues increase. One of the stewards
saw it and tore it up. I was speaking to Arnie
and said I thought what the steward did wasn't right.
Arnie says: 'No. That note was out of line.
I'm against the increase, too,
but these things should be argued
at a Union meeting, not in front of the Company.'
Larry leans over and says:
'You talk, Arnie,
as if there's two opposite sides here.'"

On Sundays, the bells of the churches:
sounds of another trade,
like the horns of the boats in Fleming Channel
bound downriver with iron ore or coal
for Ford Rouge. So many cars
with a small group of effigies on the dashboard
or the rear window shelf:
Mary, in blue and white plastic,
surrounded by plastic roses.

"Earle, the new guy, is telling us
his wife is nineteen.
'I'm glad she don't know
what we do all day,' he says.
'When I come home at night
I tell her how worn out I am
and she lets me just sit

while she gets supper.
If she knew what this job was like
she'd probably want me to help, too.'
'That's something I've wondered about,'
Brian says. 'Nothing we lift is that heavy
and we got the winches if it is.
Why don't they hire women?
It'd sure make this place more enjoyable.'
And Earle says: 'No *way*.
This is a *man's* job.' "

At lunch, by the parts desk:
"A fellow I know came home from work last week
and found his wife gone.
She took almost everything.
She only left one knife, one fork, one spoon
—like that—one plate, one cup."
And somebody else adds:
"It happened to a friend of mine, too.
And when he went into the bedroom
all his clothes were on the floor:
she left him one coat hanger."

The rain falling steadily on the pavement.

And Jim's story, about staying up Thursday night,
stoned, and punching in at work late
after just a few hours sleep.
The foreman has him in the metal shop
where the truck bodies are assembled and spot welded.
At the first break, someone remarks
how for a change that morning
none of the machines had broken down
and they hadn't been any parts short.
At this rate, the guy points out,
if nothing else went wrong they could make production
by two o'clock.
"For the next couple of hours," Jim says,
"we kept working as fast as we could.

By lunch we had trucks on every hook of the line
across most of the department. And afterwards
we went even faster. Everybody in our area
got into it: not just the longhairs
but even the immigrants and the lifers.
A couple of the guys are yelling:
Trucks. More trucks. Build more trucks.
And we're all hustling like crazy.
The foremen began to be nervous
because there was nothing for them to do.
Get out of the way, people were joking with them:
Who needs you? Go have a coffee
and come back Monday.
Then something weird happened: the foremen
start pushing the trucks *back*,
trying to slow the work down.
This was so out of character
everybody cracked up.
Hey, what are you assholes doing?
people were shouting and laughing:
Why don't you just go home?
After the last break, though,
we returned to our usual speed
and finished only half an hour early.
But it was such fun there for a while,
at the end of the day
I didn't even feel very tired."

2 *What the Women Said*

"When I told my parents
I was going to leave him
my father became enraged,
yelling out: *Whore*.
He dragged me to the window
and pointed down the street toward the jail.
That's where you're going to end up,

he shouted at me, *there
or in the nut house.* I looked at
my mother, but she left the room."

"Well, we eat at that place
because he likes Harvey's
better than McDonald's.
Depending on how hungry he is:
McDonald's when he says he's really starved."

"Working for them
is sort of a family thing.
Those of us in the office, a lot of our husbands
are out on the trucks.
The Company likes it that way
but it isn't always so good:
we work a regular eight-thirty to four-thirty
but the guys work all different shifts.
If they get off before us, sometimes they'll go drinking
and won't get home until the bar closes.
On other shifts, they're asleep all day
and when we get home they've gone to work.
We only get to see each other at breakfast."

"He came up behind
as she was crossing the parking lot by the church
with her arms full of groceries.
He got her around the neck
so she dropped the bags,
and he held a knife in front of her
and told her he'd kill her,
he'd kill her if she said anything.
All this time he was pulling her backwards
under the shadows of the trees.
He got her to sit, and knelt with her.
He kept jabbing the knife at her throat
while he pawed at her with his other hand,
exciting himself.

"All at once she tried
to catch hold of the knife, and he hit her
with his other hand, hard, in the stomach.
Then he pulled at her belt, and her jeans,
and she said she felt lost
like when your bladder let you down one day at school
or you couldn't run home fast enough.
But she started to scream
and the man took off."

"The day after we won the arbitration
and were going to get the same rate as the men,
the foreman announces
we're being transferred to another department
where—guess what?—we'll be paid at the old rate.
We sat down, refused to work,
and everything in our area came to a halt.
During the next hour or so
women and men from all over the plant
stopped by to tell us if the Company tried to fire us
or go through with the transfer
they'd walk out. But then the foreman
shows up with someone from the Union, and *he* insists
the Company has the right."

"Bruce tells me he thinks about it:
at the office, sooner or later
he works with a woman he likes, who likes him.
But he realizes, with me and the kids,
he'd be risking more than he gains.
He tries to be humorous, he says:
let her know about his attraction for her
but turn it into something they can laugh at
and so keep working together."

"My Dad, when I was fourteen,
used to put his hand down my pants all the time
and my uncle would laugh—
it was supposed to be a joke.

But I'd cry, and my mother told me:
Don't say anything to anybody; he's your father
and my uncle would, too, and my father would tell me:
If this gets beyond this house,
you're really in trouble."

> "It wasn't till years later
> when I thought about that first time
> I realized what it was: I told him, *No,*
> but he was stronger
> and we *had* been going out.
> I did like him a little, but
> not enough to do that,
> and I told him so, but he did, and
> that was the first."

"I asked him
to touch me there,
and he said: 'What's the matter?
My cock not good enough for you?' "

> "Anna says she has to clean
> and cook for her husband, their two kids,
> her cousin who boards with them—he pays
> $150 a month, meals and lodging—
> and herself. Everything has to be kept clean,
> she says, so as well as the laundry
> and the daily dishes and the floors,
> she says she does the walls every week
> and the ceiling every other week.
> All this plus the shopping and cooking,
> and some mending, and she has a job two nights a week
> selling popcorn and candy at a local theater.
> It's about eight hours a week, at the minimum wage,
> but it all helps. Just once, she says,
> she told her husband she was going on strike.
> When he got home from work
> she was over at a neighbor's:
> the breakfast dishes hadn't been done,

the house was a mess
and she didn't have supper ready.
He was furious, and came over and got her.
'I told you I was going on strike,'
she says, but he was really angry:
'He told me he'd really let me have it
if I ever did it again.' She's twenty-four."

"They got no kids
and he doesn't want her to work
so she's alone all day, and
does sewing and stuff around the house.
She tries to please, but whatever he wants
is what *she* wants, so when he asks her,
she says: "What do *you* think?"
And he gets mad: 'Don't you have a mind?'
he says."

"My brother is at home
because he got hit
by a boxcar in the yards—he works as a brakeman.
So he's relaxing
and telling everyone
how dangerous his job is.
Then I quit
because the boss is after me all the time.
'I can make things easy for you,'
he says. 'You ought to be nice to me.'
He's always grabbing me, and when I tell him
to take his hands off,
he gets mean, then the next day
starts being nice again.
It's just crazy so I left.
Now I can't get U.I. for weeks
because they say I left without a good reason.
And I'm home too,
but I don't get Compensation for what happened to me.
I can't even use that place as a reference
to find another job."

3 *Dieppe Park*

How does this change?
We who construct the City every day:
what keeps us crawling over each other
in the dark
in different directions,
certain we are going some place better?

October 14, 1976: three hundred of us wait
in Dieppe Park, here to honor the day of protest
the unions have called against the government controls
that hold our wages steady while prices rise.
Behind the speakers' platform, the Detroit River,
and on the far side of that another country:
the skyscrapers of downtown Detroit.
Finally, the spokesmen appear on stage
and Ron says to me: "Look. It's the living dead."
An old man begins to talk about the great strikes
a quarter-century ago, when all the auto plants were out
and in one action Riverside Drive was clogged with strikers' cars
—that strike won by the Union at last
with the birth of the Rand Formula.
But the crowd this morning is bored—mostly young people
impatient to march in the cold air, knowing the unions now
as something else: the activists isolated and removed
or bought off with jobs in the hierarchy;
the union protection and grievance systems
all that stands between the bosses and ourselves,
but the bureaucracy uncaring and slow
so that often only our own actions
—stoppages on the line, or walkouts,
or the threat of these—bring issues to a quick solution.
Even today, this is not a strike the unions have called
to continue until we win,
but a day off work, with tomorrow
to be the same as yesterday.

Before the last speaker is finished
we begin to move toward the road.
Dozens of union marshals are ready, however,
to ensure the march travels at a fast pace
up Ouellette and round by City Hall
and then dissolves—as though the organizers
are anxious to get this over with.

Yet there is a strike on here
against a department store chain
refusing union recognition in one of their suburban stores.
The Company has held out for months:
hundreds of people each Saturday
stream in past the pickets, to be waited on inside
by other citizens who daily cross these lines to work.
This far from the beginnings of unions,
it is as though we have to start over:
but now when someone explains
that without the founding of these organizations
we would all still work for subsistence wages,
at the whim of every company foreman—
for intolerable hours, with safety, Compensation,
unemployment payments and pensions
nonexistent, or worse than they are—
those spoken to
can point to corruption, meanness, bullying
and use these as their excuse
to cross our lines. This October day
in the crowd being hurried up the main street,
somebody suggests we march
through the downtown branch of the store.
The idea spreads with shouts, but the marshals
are quick to stop it: a group of them
take up positions in the street in front of the store's entrance
to say: *Keep moving. Keep moving.*

And at the Park, a middle-aged man
stood at the microphone for the Social Democrats.
He informs us he is our representative
in the provincial parliament, and if we re-elect him

and more like him
all will be well with us.

                    But he is nervous
as if he senses from this crowd's listless response
something here can tell he is lying.
A couple of young men not far from me
begin to heckle, and I ask myself
why do I also feel such anger?
This man is not a boss, not an owner.
Yet I do not expect
the parties of the rich to understand
what this life is like, why it has to be altered,
but this man and his party know
and they do nothing. Out of office, they talk,
and when they have been elected
they behave almost exactly
as the parties they say they oppose. They declare
they are the only alternative, they put forward a vision,
but in power, they cannot implement these things,
they explain, because the time isn't right.
"We will win more votes in the long run," they say,
"if we legislate you back to work,
if we do not institute the day care we promised.
Then, in the long run, you'll benefit
even if you lose again now."

Perhaps I loathe them
because they are that part of ourselves
that keeps us children, looking to someone other than ourselves,
bigger than ourselves, to redeem us.
This man, and the men and women like him,
see how we live
and plan to use this to get more for themselves.

And yet when we turn to each other,
many times we recognize only the powerless
and lash out: what we offer ourselves
is a human fist
smashing into a human face

—male or female—a tiny model
of what our days feel like.

                        Later this year
an unemployed auto worker with a grievance,
getting no help from the Windsor Union office,
went out to his car and returned
with a rifle, shooting, so that the staff
dived under desks or tables, or fled
to hide in washrooms and closets.
Then the man left; the rooms and hallways
suddenly quiet. But he went outside
around the building
and peered in through the windows of the executive offices
and saw Charlie Brooks under his desk
and fired through the glass and killed him.
And though what Brooks was head of
is one more organization that claims to be ours,
to speak for us, and yet so often blocks us,
at the moment Brooks was given those bullets
he was not the minister responsible for unemployment insurance,
he did not own GM.

4 *Why There Is No Calm Here*

Day and night, the huge blue trucks
of Chrysler's, and the others
climb the great iron bridge from both directions
constantly pulling
the sound across the river:
Detroit-Windsor, Windsor-Detroit.

Like the clouds
headed south out of Michigan
the trucks and trailers
travel high in the air between the cities.
But the wheels and engines
pulse at my ear, while the clouds

drift into Ontario in perfect silence.

16

5 *Recording Tachometer*

Something more
needs to be said in our lives.
At the Union local meeting
called right after work for once, the business agent
looks out at our faces and asks
if anyone has any complaints.
And nobody says a word,
but we sit heavily in the chairs
of the rented dance hall, until one man rises
and speaks about his steward, in Rigid Frame
where the trucks too large for the line are built.
He reports how the steward is dangerous to work with,
disregarding safety rules together with the foreman,
so that even the plant Safety Committee has spoken to him
yet it continues to happen. And the business agent says:
Well, you elected him. It's your problem.
Any other difficulties?

But as well as this grievance
there is the grievance of the faces:
expressed not in words
but by the young, energetic,
tossing washers at each other
all day in the plant—or, in the office,
elastic bands. And by Archie, older than the rest of the crew,
refusing to work in the area
when the vacuum attachment to the fibreglass cutter
breaks again, flooding the air here with
thousands of tiny floating particles of glass.
And Dave telling the young partsman: "Get a ladder.
Don't climb up the racks hand over hand."
And the guys on engine assembly nearby saying:
"Yeah. Slow down.
Don't you know there's an energy crisis?"

Yet despite the arguments with the foremen,
and the general foreman, the wildcats, the strikes,

17

though so many units are lost to production
or we quit,
in the end we go back
to these hours here
at the machines—which while they transform
time and materials
also do something to us.

We must begin to ask
about another life, the life we feel in the ads
for charter holidays, in the ads for clothing, stereos,
lotteries, our own cars. What happens to us
growing up, so that Bill, forty-five years old,
seeing the foreman approaching one day
when we've stopped work for a moment to talk to each other,
shouts: *Look out. Here comes the teacher.*

Someone is stealing our time, our time alive,
and all our lives are marked by that theft.
They have told us that time is money
and since money can be owned
you can possess a man or a woman's time
and spend the human beings who live in that time
like a coin or a dollar. In some trucks
we are ordered to install
a recording tachometer, so that the owners
can constantly check
on the driver: the device tells how the driver shifts,
when he stops the vehicle, how fast he was driving
at any time. So even the man alone on the highway
has the foreman watching—he remains in the factory,
like the man or woman in the bar after supper
with one eye on the clock because even off work
somebody owns your time.

                    Of course they insist
this is the only possible arrangement
whereby things can get built, the City function.
But who stands to say: *This is not good enough?*

Out of the skill and thought
we apply on the job every day
—learning how to compensate for a particular machine
to get it to produce what it is supposed to
or what we want from it,
and from our craft and decisions
which they tell us are of no particular importance
since each hour that passes is worth precisely the same
like the numbers spinning on the dials of a gasoline pump,
out of our combined accomplishments
and ideas, the change in our daily life must come.

And it is ourselves
who will have to define it and fight for it.
But it is a life
we cannot live alone: while a woman is afraid
to walk home at night, while a man or woman is desperate
for comfort or food, this time and place we share
is made worse. Out of all our imperfections,
fears, distrust, we must for our own lives
stand together against the owners of our time.

Little will improve
without this daily understanding
we have to release time itself
from its buyers and sellers.
For time, like the air,
is indivisible: where one of us is chained in time,
or has our time locked away from us,
time itself is injured—the same time
we have to live in. We have a book that says
on the seventh day a god freed time a little.
And there is our history in which we know
the struggle for eight hours won a little more.
But as long as there are wages—
so that we must obtain what we need to live
and live ourselves
according to how many pieces can be made in a day
or according to the money some hours of the day are worth—

time is still jailed, and that is the factory
we are all in.

Saturday, the Windsor air
reverberates with the noise of muscle cars, vans, pickups.
This May, in the garages by the back lanes,
snowmobiles wait for another winter of motors.

But on Monday, the high-performance cars
will be motionless
in the parking lots of the plants.
They will be silent
later today in front of the houses and apartments
where someone else goes on working at home.
In these hours, though,
the weekend tires and engines
power around town.
And all afternoon
the streets fill
with the horns of weddings.

WHITE HAND

The chain saw bites into the wood: the faller
is making the undercut
then his back cut.
And when the tree is felled
it is bucked to length,
and later the rigging crew
hauls it out to a landing.
Danger is everywhere: the rotten tops
of snags, or when a cable unexpectedly tightens
or parts, or a log slips from the grapple
and rolls. Shadowed by death, the log is carried by truck
and then perhaps to the world
of water, boomsticks and swifters
and tugs, and on to the mills.

But in the green brush
two hands stay on the chain saw
for months.
The chain cuts into the wood, the heavy saw
is lifted in, jams, is worked free
and lifted into the cut again,
for years. The constant motion
of the engine, the chain,
is sawing too
at the smallest of blood vessels
and nerves: as in the guts of a cat operator,
what in the hand of this man
is shaking free
cannot grow back—white hand,
they call it, the hand gone permanently numb,
useless...

        I take a sheet of paper
and place its sharp corners
in my typewriter roller and turn it,
and around the roller, facing my keys,

21

appears first the tip
of a man's middle finger, then the tops
of the others, so I type the poem
on the palm of a man's hand, a brother's:
white page
white hand

THE DETROIT STATE POEMS: TENNENHOUSE

A rainy morning in Detroit
and the roof of State Hall
is leaking water again into the fourth floor.
Pools form under one of the skylights
and buckets have been placed out
in the corridors. A secretary
is checking each faculty office,
making a list of those of us flooded out:
two doors along, somebody is working at his desk
wearing rubber boots; his swivel chair
rolls through an inch of water
as he wheels back to answer the phone.

                                    Money
is what the university lacks: the interior walls scarred
and dirty, like any factory, the daily office garbage here
emptied only twice a week, repairs
taking months to be attended to.

Tennenhouse sticks his head in
on his way back from an early class:

"Did I tell you, Tom, my family
originally settled near Winnipeg
when they first came from Europe?
They homesteaded, but they knew nothing
about farming; it was one of the sons who finally realized
the land they had chosen was worthless,
after years of trying. A few of my relatives
are still there, but my father
and some others moved to Detroit:
they were either going to use farm machinery
or make it. We'd have these gatherings
where the farming uncles would talk
to the auto plant uncles. The farm ones would tell about
killer hailstorms

that suddenly come up: a whole year's crop
and work ruined in a second, the stones
big enough to kill cattle
and, if you were caught in the open,
people. And the auto shop uncles
tell how sometimes a car at the end of the line
being tested will explode:
sending a hail of metal
through that part of the plant
—which is even more deadly.

"It always impressed me; it's the same
image," Tennenhouse says,
"doing either job. I guess I'm the only one of the family so far
who's really made it in out of the rain."

And he walks on down the hallway to his door
with his pipe and his books
skirting the standing water on the linoleum
and the slow drops being caught by the pails.

THE DETROIT STATE POEMS: MARKING

I begin each essay with a calm mind—
a fresh start.
But as I consider what they have written
I get angry: the most cursory of rereadings
would have caught this sentence fragment,
and here is a misused semicolon
after we spent more than an hour on that in class
and where I talked to this student individually
for another thirty minutes about this persistent mistake.
And instead of the simple structure of the expository paper
which we have also gone over and over
and which can be so helpful a model, a technique, a guide,
here again is a jumbled series of random observations:
trite, contradictory, obviously hurried
and spelled wrong.

My red pencil becomes enraged.
It stalks through the words,
precise, bitter, vindictive,
acting as if it is pleased to discover error
and pounce on it, hacking and destroying and rearranging,
furiously rooting out sloppiness and weakness
as though upholding some stern moral precept
against another, softer age.

But the hand gripping the pencil
begins to tremble with remorse.
It feels it has led the students on
to try to expresss themselves
and then betrayed them:
attacking what they have exposed
of their ideas and emotions.
What use is righteousness, the hand wishes to ask the pencil,
without charity?

I read the name at the top
and think of the young person whose effort this is.
Now all I see on the paper
is a face, crestfallen when I hand back what they attempted.
Eyes look up at me
apprehensively, as at a judge.
We both know my weighing of their skill
will be taken to be an assessment of themselves.

It is as though I have been asked to mark
not essays but their faces,
not sentences but who they are.
I raise my pencil, but my hand still shakes.
I want to show them what in normal English usage
is considered incorrect.
But I can not assign a grade to their eyes.

SURPRISES

The North Pacific surges in from the Gulf,
powerful, serenely confident,
but discovers with some amazement this is the end of the ocean:
these are inlets and not straits or passages around islands.

And on these hills, looking out to sea,
the City built itself. And here, after a while,
I came to be alive. For some years
I didn't know much: I loved the rain on the large leaves
over the streets, and on canvas
pitched on the side of nearby mountains.
I liked the water in my face on a stormy day
walking beside the beach
or along a trail through the forest.
I liked the lights switched on by one in the afternoon
at school, with the wind and rain
pushing against the big classroom windows,
making us shiver, glad for a few hours
to be where we were.

                      But with time
I learned about wages
and the price of a can of soup. Whether I nailed down
certain boards I was told to, or my pen
rasped across faint blue lines in my own room,
I could not help being startled
at what I and my friends had become.
At last, though, I was grateful
because through these friends I saw
this was the City: the tugboat deckhand,
the man on the bridge of the ferry,
the taxi driver, the prep man in a restaurant kitchen,
the housewife, the woman who scales logs
or works in a laboratory
and all the others. In their acts and mine,
in each part of our daily lives

we build this City every day—
often not the way we would like to
but as we are ordered:

                    muttering to ourselves
and telling jokes, insulting and defending it,
restless, unsure of our choices,
frustrated, impatient, laughing
and relaxed. From the ebb and flow
of our lives, the City continues,
as easy to change as to construct,
apparently not surprised
to find itself
at the edge of the ocean
sitting on its hills
filled with people like myself.

TWO STUDENTS LOOKING AT A POSTCARD OF A PAINTING BY GUSTAV KLIMT WHILE LISTENING TO GAVIN WALKER PLAY JAZZ AT THE CLASSICAL JOINT COFFEE HOUSE, VANCOUVER, B.C.

Drums again along the inlet:
two blocks south of the docks
on a rainy Thursday evening,
white man's drums
filling the room with a white rain.
At a table a young man and a young woman
here on a date begin the first touches and whispers
that will lead to another beginning with the flesh.
But now she holds onto his sweater at his chest
as she leans to put her mouth at his ear
to say something through the music.
He is the more shy of the pair.
Yet his arm touches her sweatered arm
as he bends his head almost into her hair to reply.
Her fingers stay on his shoulder;
his face is dazed with pleasure and fear.

Now Gavin Walker rises to the microphone
with his alto sax, and begins.
He is less than a meter from the two
crowded in at a front table, but the young man
sits partly turned from the music
staring down at his coffee, while the woman
watches the musicians past his face.
Gavin Walker strains at his work, his right foot
lifts from the floor
as his saxophone throws
into the steady falling white water of the drums
the notes that are harsh sparks
of reddish-brown light. At his back
the two others of his group
half-interestedly follow him: the electric bass

placing its bars of black sound
underneath the others' music, and the electric guitar
releasing from time to time into the room
its clusters of floating yellow globes.

At the table in front, the young man turns
and from the chairback pulls out of an inside pocket of his coat
a postcard of a painting by Gustav Klimt.
He lays the card flat on the table, positioned
so the young woman can see
and she bends her head to look at it too,
their hair almost touching.
It is a glittering pattern of gold and muted colors
meant to depict a woman. They do not speak.
After a few seconds
the young man takes the card from the table
and returns it to his coat again.

But now he sits with his back to her, facing the musicians.
The young woman rests her chin gently on his shoulder,
her arm around his body, holding him.
Gavin Walker finishes a solo run, but no one claps;
the drums and electric strings
drive the music forward through the night.

Before the set is over, the young man and young woman
get up to go. Gavin Walker is working again;
they have to squeeze between the microphone and the table
in order to leave. They move past him in their coats
into the wet darkness outside the door
carrying the postcard with them.

Gavin Walker does not watch them go.
It is almost midnight. He will do a slow ballad next
and then an old Miles Davis piece. After the break
he will cut the second set off short.
There are always smaller crowds on a rainy night
and this evening hardly anyone will be left in the room to hear.

NEW AND USED

after "Don Asterio Alarcón"

It's a port all right,
Vancouver, with the wind
from the harbor docks
blowing along Hastings Street
where the bottles wash up
in front of beer parlors
and short-time hotels
and paper of all kinds
drifts, and out-of-town
loggers and
sailors and miners
and the citizens
busy with their urban trades
and the police.

But a block away
at the top of Victory Park
where the men and women
sleep on the grass
is a street of
booksellers.

Here a dusty store
keeps a rack of ten-cent volumes
out by the bus stop
the way a skid-road grocery
puts spoiled broccoli and cauliflower
outside for quick sale. And two doors down
is the Party's bookshop
with news from Moscow and
Cuba and across the road
the Anglicans
sell their greeting cards and tracts.
And then at the corner

MacLeod's Books—
New and Used.

Inside, at the rear
of the dim room of floor-to-ceiling books
a man leans on a counter and stares
through to the windows in front.
And whoever old MacLeod was
and what he was like
this isn't him but the present owner
young Donald Stewart.
For all businesses like this
contain time and sell time
almost without noticing it
so one day in the quiet
MacLeod wasn't there
and Don Stewart was.

And person by person
the City stops in to see him
as they did the old man:
this one is looking
for dictionaries, and this one
for recipes, and this man
wants novels by
a certain Argentine
(in translation of course)
and here somebody
is examining the maritime section
while another peers at
Chinese history
or a few feet on railroads.

And since books
go around like money
others drop by to offer Don Stewart
school texts, or
science fiction, lurid confessions

and manuals on how to sew.
Thieves try to sell him
lavish art books
and a few orders of new editions
arrive by mail.
And always the poets appear
with their insistent
collections.

And Don Stewart
sorts through these volumes
patiently filling the holes
a day's sales make in his shelves.
He stands at the back by the cash register
like old MacLeod probably
in jeans and a grey sweater that shows
a green shirt at one elbow.

Years pass
in this shop
in silence
and a turning of pages
and Don Stewart
goes on with each day like anyone
to whom time is only
a deepening of value:
rare books becoming rarer
while the others change hands.

So when Time himself
with his scythe and hourglass
opens the door and steps in
Don Stewart will watch him
without fear or regret.
For Time is at home here
browsing among the stock.
And when he gets to the back
with a few volumes under his arm

he always meant to buy,
Don Stewart, grown old now,
will ring up his last sale
just as usual
and then the two
past the astonished customers
will go out together
talking of books.

THE FREIGHTER

The history of the Sixties?
Why not write the history of Thursday?
—Wavy Gravy (Hugh Romney), 1977

No one knows when she first appeared
to drop anchor among the dozen or more
other ships off the harbor entrance:
various sizes of freighter
here to load or unload at the City's too-few docks,
swinging round as the wind shifts.

To most people in the City
the waiting vessels are only a backdrop
if you happen to be strolling along Kits Beach
or Second Beach, or if you get a glimpse of the water
while driving to work. And at night, the lights
of these large, seagoing warehouses
are just a reminder that this *is* a seaport
—so somebody must be aware
of why each ship has arrived:
the harbormaster's office, probably,
and the Customs
or the men who run the provision boats
and the water taxis. Certainly the representatives of firms
with an interest in the vessels or their cargoes.

But one Thursday evening
an habitual beach walker
was the first amateur to notice
a certain freighter had been here a long time.

There could have been many reasons: a strike by her crew
or some difficulty with the port authorities,
but month after month the same ship remained.
Soon more people in the City
remarked on it: one vessel always present,
looming large close in to the Jericho shore

35

and seeming to shrink when relocated off Ferguson Point.
An official quoted in a City newspaper
said she was delayed due to lack of terminal space
to discharge what she carried. But a spokesman for the dock
explained she was held up pending arrival
of a shipment to take on. Both agreed
she was properly registered: American,
according to the first man, but the second insisted
she was owned by a multinational consortium.
Even casual observers sometimes argue about her:
to one person she lies deep, as though heavily loaded,
while another is sure she floats high, as if empty.
Black-hulled, with a white superstructure,
the freighter seems to have the masts and winches
of ships from decades ago.

She stays patiently offshore,
Christmas to Christmas, July to July,
through the calm weather and the storms.
And of those in the City who watch her,
most believe one afternoon
she will haul in her anchor cable and vanish.
Yet others are convinced that some morning
everyone will wake to see
that during the night she will have brought her cargo into the City

and berthed.

DAFFODILS

At a table
covered with a green cloth

on which a jar
holds freshly cut daffodils

I sit reading a book of modern Russian poems

so the heavy scent
floats through Russia,

through the lines

and among the horrifying small biographies:
the children raised in institutions
while both parents were at the front against the Nazis,
the boy living with the partisan band
that is trapped and annihilated while he watches,
the husbands or wives disappearing
through official orders

and the scent
perhaps in the air in April 1918
on Moscow's Malaia Dmitrovka Street
as the Bolsheviks suppress their Left opposition—
the gun butts of the Cheka
hammering at the door of
the House of Anarchy, each blow
ringing in another Russia:
the Factory Committees dissolved,
hammering, Kronstadt smashed,
more hammering, the Makhnovschina destroyed
—Ukrainian anarchist communes
overrun by Lenin's Army,
Bat'ko fleeing to Rumania, to Poland, then Paris—
more hammering, the pistol shot

of Mayakovsky killing himself,
the wood splintering,
a scuffle in the hallway,
blood beginning to flow across the floor

and because it is human blood
it is anarchist blood: the lash of the nobility,
the men ordered tortured and hung by the Czar,
and the men and women who thus learn
a government, even by Reds, can only be the club and the rifle.
Yet blood
is organized differently:
living according to natural laws
except that because of centuries of effort
we know it can be improved on,
altered when necessary
to benefit our life. The death camps,
the suppression of words
as harmless as poems,
and the evenings when nothing happens:
a stroll in a park somewhere
along a path amid
daffodils

      as in the wood
where the young composer was found,
May 1979, last seen entering a KGB car,
now hanging, his fingers broken,
eyes gouged out, with several branches
of the cranberry
driven into his ribs,

      daffodils
I smell here
reading these lines
in a land that isn't Paradise either.
I remember a friend saying
the twentieth century
is part of the Middle Ages.

I raise my head to look at the blossoms
on the table
and imagine later people telling each other
some things come through
from that dark era:
daffodils, for example—the bright yellow scent
unchanged, like certain words and flowers....

But these ones will never make it.

TAKING THE DEAD OUT OF MY ADDRESS BOOK

Jeff Marvin

In the cold days before the New Year
I am taking the dead out of my address book.

I pass a line through the names.
Some were the parents of friends,
one was buried deep in the earth,
another burned in the air.
Now word has come of one
caught between the sky and the ground,
frozen far down a crevice,
suspended, too difficult to hook
and pull up.

While this happened
my address book went on carrying them
like a tree that keeps its dead leaves
hung as dusty rags
all winter.

When I get a new book
there will be no trace on its pages
that these people lived
—like lovers or friends
who after years we never see.
My name
meantime is written and vanishes
in other people's pages, too,
rehearsing the moment
it will disappear
forever.

At the printers,
men and women watch the machines
turn out sheets of ruled paper,
ready to be trimmed and bound,
to hold names.

And further off is a mountain
covered with white snow.

from
THE FACE OF JACK MUNRO
(1986)

HAMMER

A hammer is rising. A hammer
thrown up at the end of the day by a carpenter
with blood on the handle where his blisters have been.
A hammer. It lifts as well on the wave of steam
pouring up from the pots of a kitchen—a tiny kitchen
of an apartment, and that of a restaurant
serving a hundred customers at once.

A great cry of tedium
erupting out of papers and fluorescent glass
carries the hammer higher. It goes up end over end
on a tune broadcast to a million people.
And it climbs
on the force of a man's arm alone
flung straight up from the sickness that is his life.
It rises out of the weight of a body falling.

Nothing can stop it. The hammer has risen for centuries
high as the eaves, over the town. In this age
it has climbed to the moon
but it does not cease rising everywhere each hour.
And no one can say what it will drive
if at last it comes down.

PAPER, SCISSORS, STONE

An executive's salary for working with paper
beats the wage in a metal shop operating shears
which beats what a gardener earns arranging stone.

But the pay for a surgeon's use of scissors
is larger than that of a heavy equipment driver removing stone
which in turn beats a secretary's cheque for handling paper.

And, a geologist's hours with stone
nets more than a teacher's with paper
and definitely beats someone's time in a garment factory with scissors.

In addition: to manufacture paper,
you need stone to extract metal to fabricate scissors
to cut the product to size.
To make scissors you must have paper to write out the specs
and a whetstone to sharpen the new edges.
Creating gravel, you require the scissor-blades of the crusher
and lots of order forms and invoices at the office.

Thus I believe there is a connection
between things
and not at all like the hierarchy of winners
of a child's game.
When a man starts insisting
he should be paid more than me
because he's more important to the task at hand,
I keep seeing how the whole process collapses
if almost any one of us is missing.
When a woman claims she deserves more money
because she went to school longer,
I remember the taxes I paid to support her education.
Should she benefit twice?
Then there's the guy who demands extra
because he has so much seniority
and understands his work so well

he has ceased to care, does as little as possible,
or refuses to master the latest techniques
the new-hires are required to know.
Even if he's helpful and somehow still curious
after his many years—
again, nobody does the job alone.

Without a machine to precisely measure
how much sweat we each provide
or a contraption hooked up to electrodes in the brain
to record the amount we think,
my getting less than him
and more than her
makes no sense to me.
Surely whatever we do at the job
for our eight hours—as long as it contributes—
has to be worth the same.

And if anyone mentions
this is a nice idea but isn't possible,
consider what we have now:
everybody dissatisfied, continually grumbling and disputing.
No, I'm afraid it's the wage system that doesn't function
except it goes on
and will
until we set to work to stop it

with paper, with scissors, and with stone.

THE SOUND: FACTORY SYSTEM POEM

The moment the hooter goes
I reach for the small cardboard case in my toolbox
and tear off a tuft of cotton
to plug in each ear.

Before the shift starts,
in the low sounds of people clocking in,
getting changed and standing around drinking coffee
and talking, or reading the paper, the first aid man
puts a dozen new packages of ear cotton
on a table in his room
for anybody who has run out.

If I don't use it, the noise
doesn't seem so bad at the start
with rivets being hammered, the hiss of
air hoses, the shouts, engines, the pounding.
Yet as the first hours pass, the sound
begins to echo in my ear:
never deafening
but a steady high-pitched drilling
I'm always aware of.

                    Even with the cotton
I touch my ear to make sure the plugs are in place
when a router or winch seems especially loud.
The fibre
itches a little constantly
but if I take it out for a second
when I put the cotton back it's like on a hot day
when you dive under the surface of a sunlit lake
into the cool and quiet.

             Speech
is audible almost unchanged:
people making suggestions, or jokes,

and what the foreman says to do next.
Occasionally I have to ask someone to talk louder, though.
A few guys wear Mickey Mouse ears—the headphones
which function the same as cotton.
But since the Company doesn't provide these
most of us stick with what we're given.

Yet if they could make an ear protector
so powerful that when we wore it
there was absolute silence,
a voice
would still speak continually here in the din
saying:

            a factory is not a tool
for production, like a screwdriver
or the compressed air impact wrench.
It is a way of organizing people
to do a job, human beings
who are supposed to follow orders
and not argue, perform
and not comment. There can be no such thing as
a socialist factory
any more than a left-wing, interest-charging bank
or a Red army. These structures, hierarchies
belong to another age
and have to be altered, dismantled, rebuilt
to improve them
for as long as they can't be shut down.
But they will never
be ours.

LECTURE

We sit in rows
facing a man
who is talking. We
are not saying anything.
Suddenly a door near the back
opens
and most of us turn our heads.

Is someone
from a
different life
about to enter?
Will he or she bring
the air from outside
tasting of the sea,
spices and malt,
fresh-cut planks?
Will it be a person
who can articulate
why we are uneasy
in this room,
fearful of complaining
when what is said
is unsatisfactory?

Whoever is entering
is in the door now
and we observe
she is
only one of us,
nervous at arriving late,
hurriedly taking a seat.
Our heads
swivel again
silently to where the talker
has continued

50

with his words
all this time.
Maybe he
will deliver us, break
into song, reveal wonders,
make our presence in this
cramped room
worthwhile. But it looks
doubtful.

Toward the rear, a door opens.

STUDENTS

The freshman class-list printouts
showed birthdates so recent
Wayman was sure the computer was in error.
One young man, however, was curious
about Wayman's mention near the start of term
of his old college newspaper:
"You were an editor *when*? Wow,
that's before I was born."

The wisdom of the students
hadn't altered, though.
Wayman observed many clung to
The Vaccination Theory of Education
he remembered: once you have had a subject
you are immune
and never have to consider it again.
Other students continued to endorse
The Dipstick Theory of Education:
as with a car engine, where as long as the oil level
is above the add line
there is no need to put in more oil,
so if you receive a pass or higher
why put any more into learning?

At the front of the room, Wayman sweated
to reveal his alternative.
"Adopt The Kung Fu Theory of Education,"
he begged.
"Learning as self-defence. The more you understand
about what's occurring around you
the better prepared you are to deal with difficulties."

The students remained skeptical.
A young woman was a pioneer
of The Easy Listening Theory of Learning:

spending her hours in class
with her tape recorder earphones on,
silently enjoying a pleasanter world.
"Don't worry, I can hear you,"
she reassured Wayman
when after some days he was moved to inquire.

Finally, at term's end
Wayman inscribed after each now-familiar name on the list
the traditional single letter.
And whatever pedagogical approach
he or the students espoused,
Wayman knew this notation would be pored over
with more intensity
than anything else Wayman taught.

ARTICULATING WEST

In May
I shook the prairie dust
out from under my tires
and took the route
over the Kicking Horse
and Rogers Pass,
meeting wet snow once
that day high in the forest,
and once hail,
until, descending,
at
Revelstoke
I ran into green:
the twelve different shades of green
and of yellow
in the springtime woods—
alder trees, the ferns and underbrush
and even fresh green
on the tips of the evergreen spruce.
And I rolled down the highway
filling my lungs with
the good green air, until near Sicamous
I turned off to follow the Shuswap River
deeper into the green: along that road
the lilac was in violet blossom
and the apple in white blossom
and each green farm
tucked in among the green hills
had its small orchard
of peaches or cherries.
And the green interior
of my green car
began to sprout: little woody shoots
appeared on the dashboard
and winding out of the handbrake handle,
tendrils and stalks and unfolding leaves

poking out of the glove compartment
and around the edges of the floor mats.
The steering wheel in my fingers
started to have the feel of fibre
and through the leaves now framing
the windshield
I could see the front of the car
disappearing into foliage.
Everywhere around me in the vehicle
plastic and metal
were becoming earth; the empty seat beside me
was now a flower bed
with roses and rhododendrons
about to open.
But the car's ride
began to be rough
and I poked my head through the laurel hedge
growing up the outside of the door
and saw the tires were no longer rubber
but looked more like tree trunks
forming around the spinning axles.
Thus, as I pulled into Vernon
the motor by this time halting and uneven too
I only just managed to locate John Lent's house
and turn up his driveway
where at the foot of his great green lawn
the entire construction that had been an automobile
stopped, and the sides
fell away like a cracked flowerpot
so I was left sitting
in a pleasant arbor
the stem of a young tree in my hand
and here were John and Jude coming smiling down the lawn
and all I could say
by way of explanation
was:
I'm home.

MOTION PICTURES

Of all locations to park, my car prefers
country drive-in theatres:
those fields fenced off in the dusk
echoing with the noise of speakers attached to poles
where every vehicle faces the same way
except a few pickups
containing hardy individuals settled down in the back
under coats and blankets.

                     My car especially enjoys
films about characters on the road
that include travelogue sequences as filler:
shots of strange North American cities
or European landscapes my car will never visit.
My car likes to observe these distant places
without having had to roll that far,
pistons rising and plunging,
all systems functioning, alert
for any failure.
What my car isn't happy about
are chase scenes: vehicles smashing
together, or swerving onto sidewalks
or down embankments to end in flames.
My car has passed too many overturned trucks
and police flares at other accidents
to successfully remind itself this is just a movie.
And my car seems indifferent
if the plot involves only people
indoors. But when this occurs
it loves to look higher than the screen
and the hills around,
up at the massed stars,
and recollect certain nights

it spent away out on the earth
in gear and travelling.

               My car is always a little regretful
when the films conclude
and it has to get in line
down the usual hard highway.

COUNTRY FEUDS

Out of town, disagreements between neighbors
are as simple as water:
water rights, diversion of creeks,
water lines
or shared wells that go dry. The feuds
grow naturally as animals:
grazing someone's cows
in return for a spring calf
or whether a quarter of a hog
is equal to a quarter of a heifer
in the fall. Some arguments
root deep in the purpose
of the country: people who want to operate
a small sawmill on their acreage
and the folks across the lane who moved here
for the quiet.

       Each winter
the troubles become more intense.
Somebody stops speaking to certain friends
whenever they meet in the village
and much later a phone call is made
Hey, are we having a quarrel?
If so, we can really get behind it.
And if not, don't be so surly when we see you.
These winter hassles are not limited
to a few miles of road. Strange letters to officials
—local, regional and national—
get written in the early darkness
on country tables
and mailed.

       At any season
you must be careful what you say.
Tree farm licences,
road access, ducks' eggs

versus chickens',
when carrots are tastiest and should be picked
—all can be tests. In each home
is a list, continually updated,
of which acquaintances are assets
and which liabilities, what stands on specific issues
are to be condemned.
An outsider or newcomer is allowed a few mistakes
but visitors who persistently express wrong opinions
or inquire too often after a name
currently not mentioned on this property
are subject to classification themselves.

To avoid these disputes
you have to stay in the city. Once you turn off the highway
onto dirt roads
you are headed
for a fight.

BREATH: FOR FRED WAH

you know
these mountains breathe
from below   from the valleys:
they breathe in
and Fall
floats down at noon
in the wooded hills
over the Lake
first snow on ridgelines
descends;

      breathe out
and Spring
rises from gravel
up the yellowing slopes
between evergreens   the wind
at first with the glaciers in it
and then sun;

      breathe out
sounds of the Lake
flowing against docks
and the rocky shore   air
tosses the willow-tops'
strands and branches   as seaweed
on a choppy day
birch leaves, cottonwood
vibrate
in the breezy light
glints on the moving water—

     the Lake
surges uphill
through the new leaves

you see

RAISING A RELATIONSHIP

It starts as two people enjoying themselves.
Months later, one of them gets a bit moody
and the other asks: "What's wrong?"
"Nothing," the first replies
but the other insists: "That's not true."
Then the first says: "I wasn't certain to begin with
but now I am. I checked and
whether you like it or not
we're having a relationship."
A silence. The first again:
"Of course, if you don't want to
I can always get rid of it."
A longer silence. Then the other:
"No, it's just...rather unexpected. But,"
cheering up,
"if you think about it,
it's marvellous." The two embrace
and life continues almost as before.

Except slowly the responsibility involved
becomes evident. One of the pair
out for a night on the town
decides to cut the evening short
because the other is home alone with the relationship.
Arguments now must be settled
with a minimum of fuss
for the relationship's sake.
Purchases are made on this basis, too.
"Let's go to Hawaii in December.
That'll be good for the relationship."
Various people aren't seen as often
due to their negative influence on the relationship.

And should the couple separate
there's the problem of custody.
Often one wants to keep it

and tries to convince the other to show more interest
though they are living apart.
Or, neither wishes it around in their new lives
and their friends become concerned
at how breezily the two fend off questions
about what happened to it.
Sometimes both would like the relationship
but don't want to be with each other
—which leads to a lot of confusion
as they attempt to sort this out.
Such uncertainty can drag on
until the relationship grows up and leaves on its own
determined, after all these years,
to have some fun.

from
**IN A SMALL HOUSE
ON THE OUTSKIRTS OF HEAVEN**
(1989)

ONE LUMP OR TWO

In your sugar bowl, *Frank said*,
sugar gets hard and sticks to the sides.
It's no different in the various silos
at the Spreckels mill.
Three of us are lowered on ropes
into a silo each shift,
dressed in a sort of moon suit
with pickaxe and shovel.
For the next eight
we pry the sugar from the walls.

Each time when I touched bottom
I'd say to myself: "It's a small step
for a man, but a giant leap
for the working class." The foreman
never went down. He's supposed to stay on top
to watch our ropes
but he regularly takes off somewhere.
Anyway, nobody bothers to be hauled up
when we have to take a piss.
We just let fly where we stand.
I stopped using sugar much when I got that work.

They had us on rotating shifts
which I didn't like.
But graveyards were best.
I or somebody would carve a bed
in the sugar, out of the foreman's line of vision.
We'd usually manage
to each grab a few hours sleep during the night.

Strangest part of the job, though,
was my boots. No matter how clean they looked
when I took them off
or where in the house I left them
they'd both be completely covered with ants
when I'd go to put them on for work again.

THE BIG THEFT

for Howard White

It's one of those myths
from the workplace, told by somebody who is sure
the story is true. So you believe it, until

you find yourself listening to another version
of the tale. In this case
let's call it The Big Theft. I first heard it
in a truck assembly plant:

before you came, Tom, there was a guy,
Roger Hutchison, worked here:
an oldtimer. The guard caught him
at the gate one afternoon
leaving with an oil pressure gauge in his lunchkit.
Hell, we all take something home
if we can use it—clips or seat cushions—
Roger was just unlucky and got nabbed.
But for some reason they went around to his house
and discovered a nearly completed truck
in his garage. Over the years, he had boosted
piece by piece almost everything for it.
He'd obviously gotten help moving the larger items
like the frame or the engine
from the parts yard. But he had built
pretty damn close to an entire tractor unit
in his spare time.

        Then at coffee
on a renovation job:
Donny used to be employed at a brickworks
where a man each day
took a brick home in his lunchbox.
Only one brick. But when the man dropped dead of a heart attack
the week before he was due to retire
they found he had stockpiled

a few bricks less than the total he needed
to construct his dream house.

How this myth began isn't hard to grasp.
Even the dullest among us can understand
no amount of money the company pays
really compensates for the time and effort
the job takes out of our lives.
As the slogan says: *the things we give up*
to go to work
are never returned. It's pleasant to imagine
some person someplace turning the tables.

And as with every myth, there's a lesson here.
This teaches we can gain possession
of what we make where we are employed
but not by acting alone.

Plus it is evident
rent-a-cops aren't posted at the office door at quitting time
to check the executives' briefcases
or certain envelopes addressed to the owners.
If these containers were opened
inside would be revealed
part of the value of the labor we perform each shift
being snuck out past the fence.
What these people remove secretly
isn't material required on the job
so they don't consider their actions stealing.
Yet from our work
a group of men and women get richer than us
without even asking us to vote
on whether we consent to this situation.
And that's
no myth.

WHY PART-TIME STAFF DON'T RECEIVE PRORATED BENEFITS

for Jack Finnbogason

We don't require people. Instead,
we identify specific functions to be performed.
Consider a sessional: employed, say,
to teach geography. We can use her throat
where the vocal cords are, but not her teeth.
Why should we pay part of a dental plan?
If I purchase a chalkboard from a dealer
I don't also have to buy a desk they're offering for sale.

You argue that because someone
has a clerical job with us six hours a day
we should contribute six-eighths of
his or her medical premiums. But these employees
have complete use of their bodies
for the eighteen hours a day we have absolutely no control
over what they do.
Rather than extend coverage to part-time help
our immediate goal in negotiations is to reduce
payment of full-time employees' benefits
to a fairer level: from one hundred per cent
to eight twenty-fourths.
You can see how reasonable this is.
Whatever damage the staff cause to their health
during their hours off work
should be their responsibility.
I hope you'll agree, too, this is merely a first step
toward establishing a more equitable arrangement.
Next we intend to calculate
how many days each month an employee isn't present
—sick time, weekends and holidays, for instance—
and take these into account
in determining our share of coverage.

That is what we should be discussing
when we talk about prorated benefits.
Such a change makes better use
of the institution's financial and human resources.
Don't we both want this? To minimize expenses
while spending the dollars we have most efficiently?
Which is why our plan for the long term
is to hire the majority of non-managerial personnel
only for certain targeted skills.
This policy allows for more flexibility
in meeting the demands of the market.
We must realize the era of the full-time employee
—except for executives—has passed.
And if the part-timers object to
the thrust of our current operational strategy
they should remember: individuals like them
have just a casual involvement here.
Believe me, those of us with a total commitment to this place
understand best what it needs.

A CURSING POEM: THIS POEM WANTS GORDON SHRUM TO DIE

1971

This poem wants to hurt another person.
This poem wants another person to die.
It wants him to suddenly stumble
feel a sharp pain just under the belly
a harsh pain, one that rips him so hard inside that he shits himself.
The poem wants him to become dizzy
feel a rush of sweat on the face
to begin to shiver, and have to be helped into bed.
The poem wants his teeth to chatter, wants him to throw up
gasping for air, wants mucus to pour from his nose and mouth.
It wants him to die in the night.

This poem wants Gordon Shrum to die.
First because despite all his company's rules and tariffs
despite every regulation they tell the press they apply
his company turned off the heat and light in the house.
They did this without warning, when the temperature was forty
    degrees by day
and the nights begin at four o'clock.
So that after working all day, the body could come home
to a room of black ice.
So after straining all day at the jobsite, with the fingers
numb at the hammer and slipping under the weight of the heavy
    boards
after the back was twisted trying to hoist the load of a wheelbarrow
the rest of the body could return to darkness and cold.

This poem also wants Gordon Shrum to die
because his company charges twenty-five cents every day
for the bus to carry you to work. And because you must
pay the same every evening to wait in the cold
to be jerked and stopped and jerked and stopped
all the way back to the house. Fifty cents a day
taken out of the dollars squeezed from the body's labor

so at the end of the day, the body can be hauled to where it stays
    overnight
can enter the black bedrooms, be lit by a candle
and eat bread and cold milk.

Lastly the poem wants Gordon Shrum to die
because at a meeting he reached over to my friend Mark Warrior
and smacked him in the mouth.
He was charged and duly acquitted
because Mark was shouting out at the time how the French
were finally getting off their knees
and striking back at the bullies that push them, at the men like Shrum
—whom Mark didn't name.

But whom I name, with his bureaucrats and service division
his credit office and transportation system. Him, and
every other animal who is gnawing away at our lives.
May before they die
they know what it is like to be cold, may the cold eat into them
may they live so they cough all night and can't sleep
and have to get up the next morning for work just the same.
May the joints of their bodies swell with their labor
and their backs ache. And before they die
may they know deeply, to the insides of their stomachs
the meaning of a single word:
unemployment. May they understand it
as the nourishment a man gets by scraping the calendar over a pan for
    a meal.
May they have a future with nothing in it
but unemployment; may they end on welfare.

May they have to travel by bus
to get their welfare. May they wake in the night and realize
that for the rest of their lives they will never eat together
all the things they love: steak and wine and hot corn.
They will never have these together again until they die.
May they die on welfare.
And may the Lord God *Jesus* have mercy on their souls.

MARSHALL-WELLS ILLUMINATION

for Jim Daniels

One bright morning, I was sent
to the wholesale cash-and-carry hardware,
glad to be out of the pounding and saws
of the jobsite, to drive the city streets
and walk into the wooden-floored building.

At the counter, the lone clerk
I had spoken with several times before
—an old man, surely past retirement—
fussed at his order books, precise
as his usual shirt and tie
concerning *common* or *finishing*
galvanized or *not*,
lengths and amounts needed.
The stock numbers were passed
to somebody else for fulfillment
and I stood waiting, in my workclothes and boots.
Motes of dust
rose and drifted in the sunlight
that leaned in from windows down the long room
where a dozen other people toiled at desks.
Then a man entered
from outside, older than me,
younger than the clerk, dressed in coveralls
and leather carpenter's apron.
He pulled a list from a pocket
and stepped aside, as the counter clerk
bent once more to flip the pages of the catalogs
to set the number of each item
on the proper form.

And the man in coveralls
perhaps for pleasure at the new day,
suddenly shifted his heavy boots back and forth

in a clumsy part of a dance
and stopped, grinning.

The motion caught the clerk's eye, and he frowned.
But the man
stomped his boots
in another quick pattern. He paused
under the clerk's dour gaze,
then resumed: the thick soles toeing the planks
and tipping back on heels,
nails falling from the pouches of his apron
as his arms flew out for balance. The man,
laughing, looked over at me for approval.
And the clerk also faced in my direction
shaking his head to invite me to mock
the ridiculous swaying.

                                    But at this moment
        I knew
neither gravity nor
centrifugal force
spins the Earth through space.
Our planet revolves
under the dancing feet of this man
and those like him: through their efforts
the immense bulk of our home
is moved. And I understood
as the boots crashed down, this joy
finds even in the dreadful agreements we labor in
the love required to trample
what we have been given
under our invincible shoes.

                                    Yet the three of us
hung suspended
in the amber light:
Grandfather Paper and Order,
Father Happiness and Measuring Tape

and myself. The rest of the office watched us
from their file drawers and typewriters
as I saw the planet lurch forward
with each kick of these feet
and the earth also pushed on
by the weight of an invoice
dropped from an aged hand, saw Father and Grandfather
both turned
to ask me to choose
—one motionless, the other beginning to slow.

What could I do
but dance?

THE POET MILTON ACORN CROSSES INTO THE REPUBLIC OF HEAVEN

Somewhere west of his death, he stood
before a tall cottonwood or alder.
As on an autumn afternoon, the leaves
had turned to luminous yellows, shaking
in a wind, the motions of blades and stems
at times swaying to a unified falling and lifting
then back into hundreds of different flurries.

The walls of a bluff or canyon
rose behind the tree. And he saw
high in the branches
or the air, an energy
made visible, a cloud
drifting toward him.
When it touched ground, it took the form
almost of a person
blurred by a light emanating from itself
although appearing to be dressed in a white gown
with waist-length wings.

He was determined not to be awed
by anything metaphysical.
His hand reached for the shirt pocket
where he usually kept his cigars. Nothing.
"You're an angel?" he asked, gruffly as he could.
Despite himself, his voice sounded nervous
to his ears. *No*. The sweet accent
was neither male nor female.
This is a shape meant to be familiar to your species.

His hand shook slightly
as he patted his other shirt pocket.
Empty. He cleared his throat.

"As a dialectical materialist," he said,
"I have to tell you
your wings are too short.
I read once for a human-size body to stay airborne
its wings would need to be pretty damn large."
The figure in front of him shimmered.
While he strained to focus, the figure's wings
extended to reach the dusty soil.

"Much better," he said, attempting to keep the initiative.
"You wouldn't have a cigar on you?"
No response. He shrugged.
"Well, if you aren't an angel, are you a saint?
St. Peter, perhaps? Ready to judge if I'm worthy to pass
the Pearly Gates?" He jabbed out a finger.
"I never believed in
any afterlife. I used to say I wouldn't want to spend eternity
with any of the pious frauds and criminals
they're always telling us on Earth
get to go to Paradise."

There is only one life, the figure said.

"Then how is it I'm speaking with you?"
he replied. A cold gust shook the leaves.
The poet shivered.

Do you feel you merit an everlasting existence?
The figure's voice was curious.

"If I had to, I could testify to God himself
—or herself, come to think of it—
I was honest,
true to my class, my country, my art.
I was a good carpenter,
a builder first with wood, then words.
I spoke out for what I believe.
I shouted, 'Love!'"

Some days your mind fogged,
the figure said gently.
It wasn't your fault. But evil and good,
master and victim
became confused for you toward the end. You roared
at the helpless as well as the guilty.

Then he remembered
events he could not know before
and he felt ashamed.
After some moments, he muttered:
"I worked with what I had, didn't I?"

It's unimportant now, the figure said.
Those things occurred in history. Here
you are out of time.
Soon you will abandon
the personality you grew, forever.

A gust sent some of the intense yellow leaves
spiralling from the branches.

"Then why this talk?" he asked, bitterly.
"I thought when I died I would just disappear.
This is cruel: to bring me back
for a stupid chat. To have to die again.
I was disappointed by much when I was alive.
I never dreamed I would be disappointed by death."

It's cruel to be born, the figure said.

"Don't give me crap!" he replied.
Then, calmer,
"If it's going to end for me now,
actions speak louder than words.
Let me see God."

What? The figure sounded astonished.

"Yeah, if there really is one.
I want to make sense
of what happened, of meeting you.
That would make more of this fit together."

If you want to see God, you can,
the figure said.
And where the figure had been
a shape contracted
and swirled away, as if smoke,

so the poet saw the great tree
with the wind
like all the winds of the world
stirring the golden leaves.
Then stillness in the branches.
Then a wind again.

That is God, the voice of the figure said
from the air.

And as the poet watched the tree breathe,
he entered
the republic of the dark.

IN A SMALL HOUSE ON THE OUTSKIRTS
OF HEAVEN

after Zbigniew Herbert

In a small house on the outskirts of Heaven
I met the poet. He was on crutches,
one leg in a cast, angry as ever.
"I thought we were raised up in the body
whole and perfect," I said to soothe him.
What a joke, he agreed, bitterly. *But if you head downtown*
you can find all that fairy-tale nonsense:
streets of gold and people with perfect complexions
and gorgeous robes, lazing around as if their sole concern
is to improve their technique on the harp.
That's not for the majority, though.
I broke this leg when I slipped on a ladder
at the jobsite. They're expanding the suburbs like crazy.
Most of the new housing is for people like us;
it's junk I'm ashamed to help build.

This bungalow was unfinished outside
with white siding covering the bottom half of the walls
and the rest still insulation paper. Steep stairs
led from the front walk to the main floor.
The yard was mounds of dirt
and piles of scrap lumber. A battered tricycle
was tipped over near a heap of sand
on which was a toy bulldozer minus one tread
and a plastic boat.

                    "Somebody else lives here?"
I asked. *I rent the upstairs,* the poet said.
A single mother is in the basement.
It's a horrible way to have to raise a kid.
"You pay rent?" I said. "You have to earn a living?
This isn't how I imagined Heaven to be."
You thought the rich would suffer for their crimes?
he blustered. *The poor would be rewarded?*

Not in this universe. The Old Authoritarian
likes everything as it is. Life here is exactly as fair
as where we came from. We had it correct when we were alive:
make things more just on Earth
and you improve Heaven, too.

"You mean there's no hope?"
This ain't Hell, he said sharply. *Of course there's hope.*
He poled himself across the room
and gently lifted a cat off some papers on a chair.
A few of us have begun to hold meetings.
Look. Started our own paper.
We're exposing conditions in the building trades.
Worse than any non-union job you ever worked.
Nobody has to put up with this,
not once they understand they're entitled to better.
Two bits.

      "Two bits?" I said.
Yeah, he said, thrusting the paper toward me.
I have to ask you to pay for it,
otherwise we won't be able to keep publishing.
I'm laid off with this leg
and Compo in this place is as big a laugh as on Earth.
"I don't have any money," I said.
"I've only been here a short while."
Then take it. He passed me the sheets of newsprint
and swiveled to rummage among the other papers on the chair.
Got some back issues, too.
Pay me when you can. He straightened
and turned to face me, both hands full.
We're having a picket tomorrow. Our first action
as a group, where one of our members works.
We have to be at the factory by six-thirty a.m.
He held out a leaflet.
See you there?

DEFECTIVE PARTS OF SPEECH: OFFICIAL ERRATA

Where it says *welfare* read *suffering*
"The seasonally-adjusted rate of suffering
fell one per cent last month."
Where it says *defense* read *suffering*
"The Department of Suffering confirmed Friday
the shipment of $1 billion in new tanks and helicopters
to friendly governments in Latin America."
Where it says *productivity* read *suffering*
"Canadian industry must increase the suffering of its employees
at least 12 per cent this year."
Where it says *co-operation* read *suffering*
"The administration requires the suffering of every citizen
to see us through these difficult times."

Where it says *efficiency* read *suffering*
Where it says *management* read *suffering*
Where it says *suffering* read *defeat*

DEFECTIVE PARTS OF SPEECH:
HAVE YOU REALLY READ ALL THESE?

A wall of books in my house: a giant page of words
made from multicolored letters
formidable

        to some
who have learned instead or
also to read
water, for example
in the bay
with a southeast wind
how the currents and fish respond

or the park warden looking at sign
See? The coyote have been eating the deer.

Ernie Frank stopping where the trail has exposed
soil horizons, showing us
what they reveal

Or the mountain guide explaining
how he interprets snow: the amount the crystals tell
by their shape and dampness

You think we didn't have clocks?
the elder asked Sandy Cameron
*The tide was our clock. We understood
the time of day and day of the year
from the tide.*

And the people who decipher accurately
the face of those they love
or hate

My insurance agent who insists
I know who is most likely to have a car accident
by how they walk into this office.

Men and women who study
the world
picking up warnings and
diagnoses, remedies
and fables

—all these
and more

DEFECTIVE PARTS OF SPEECH: HIERARCHY

A trout propels itself through water
with a lamprey dangling from its side.
Because the fish does not remember, its lamprey
seems natural as its tail.
The fish long ago learned to correct
for the extra shape and weight
as it swims.

If you watch the fish's eyes
there is no sign it is aware
it is being eaten alive.
The fish part of this dual organism
continues trying to survive and prosper
as a fish. If it sees
a being identical with itself
but without the parasite embedded in its flesh,
draining it,
that too seems ordained:
some of us have this appendage,
others don't
If it notices a fish
with four or five lampreys
suspended, the rasps of their teeth
sunk into its belly and face
so that fish has become immobile,
listlessly gulping water,
ready to die,
the thought is
there's a sick
one of us
If further reasoning were possible
the extra observation might be
that fish grew more of these limbs
than I did
But the concept never flashes
into the brain
and the still-useful host
darts away.

HATING JEWS

How much work
it must be to despise the Jews.
Fourteen million people, or more:
a majority of whom you've never met
but every one
has to be hated. Anti-Semites surely deserve some credit
for undertaking this colossal task.

And speaking of Semites, what about women and men
who hate Arabs? There are more Arabs
than Jews: some who dwell in the desert
and can't read or write,
some who ride around in air-conditioned limousines
rich as Jews are supposed to be.
What an effort is required
to detest so many social groups:
urban, nomads, electronic
specialists, nurses, irrigation technicians.

Meantime, certain individuals
loathe Orientals. I think these haters
should receive an international prize
for their willingness to abhor such a high percentage
of their own species. But others
hate homosexuals
or lesbians, or all men
or women—the latter two projects
being probably the largest ever initiated
in human history.

Yet having an aversion
only to Jews
is such a mammoth endeavor
no wonder those who tackle it
look drained: faces twisted, body slumped.

A few pros after years of training
carry it off more comfortably.
But ordinary women and men who sign up for this activity
seem to my eyes heavily burdened.

And me? I am repulsed
by those human beings who do me harm.
I'm not as ambitious as
the big-league despisers, though.
I attempt to focus my disgust
on specific individuals
causing pain to myself or my friends.
It's true I've learned to dislike
some general classifications of people
—for example, landlords and employers.
But rather than loathe each one of them
I try to remember the source of their odiousness
is the structure that gives them
their power over me
and aim my rage at that.

So I'm not against hate. I consider some of it
excellent for the circulation: enough injustice
remains on this planet
to justify hate being with us a while yet.
My intent is
to see it directed
where it will do the most good.

GREED SUITE: THE SKELETON

Greed has its shadow.
A bloated person gorging
herself or himself
projects behind
the shape of a skeleton.
No matter how furiously
the greedy eat—choking down handfuls of abundance,
sweeping armloads more along the table toward themselves,
the shadow by their chair
remains gaunt.
Flights to sunny beach resorts
across thousands of kilometres of water
cannot shake this companion.
Far below the aircraft, skimming the ocean surface
is the dark outline
of bones.

The shadow is not linked
to these men and women
at the soles of their feet. Rather, the skeleton begins
at the head.
Thus a skull's
damp, earthen breathing
rhythmically cools the skin of their faces.
Despite living so close to darkness
they insist they do not understand
why they are joined to the grisly being.

But the spectre dims their happiness.
The amount they own does not make them joyous,
at ease, good to others.
All they swallow piles up
as bitter yellow fat
around the heart.
They sometimes boast such plumpness is
insulation from the world.

Yet their possessions do not free them
from desiring more
or from anger at the poor,
at the poor's obstinate hunger.
And to have this frightening silhouette
trail them as if a result
of their wealth
they consider unfair.

GREED SUITE: THE SALMON

for Terry Glavin

In October, in the waters of the Gulf
the salmon circle.
More than two million pinks and sockeye
swim in a great turning wheel.
For the first time in memory, the fish have balked
at entering the Fraser River,
the mouth that leads back
to where they were born,
where they would spawn and die
in the tributaries of the Thompson River
and Adams Lake, the Bonaparte and
Nicola watersheds. Biologists in helicopters
and boats
hover over the immense ring
that has appeared off Sand Heads.
These men and women talk of
changes in sea currents
or genetic mutations. But no one is sure if,
instead, the salmon recall
their birth-grounds choked
with stumps and branches, with soil
carried down by the runoff
that is also a consequence of logging.
Or if they remember that the coastal estuaries
where as fingerlings they paused
to acclimatize themselves to ocean
are polluted and blocked.
Or has some chemical trigger
detectable in the fish's brain
informed them that the river
holds less water this season than ever before?
And thus the stone projections
behind which the salmon moving upstream need to rest
are now above the surface
as are the fish-ladders that men constructed

so the salmon could pass the rubble
blasted by the railroad builders into the canyons?

Do the salmon comprehend
the river had to shrink
and spawning creeks be destroyed
because the fiscal year has entered the food chain?
Are they able to understand
that the dams of the power corporation
have eaten too much water?
Certain authorities could at least
order spillways opened.
In far cities, though, women and men carrying briefcases
battle up the levels of the hierarchy
to find the right office to
spawn paper and words.
These visitors offer presentations
on the economic marginality of commercial fishing
and the importance to the nation
of the financial health of their *own* firms.
So the ministries announce a program
to study the issue.

              Yet beyond the river delta
salmon continue to arrive from the Pacific
to school together
like an enormous silent protest rally
outside a seat of government.
Occasionally, however,
a thousand or more of the most desperate fish
spin away from the huge revolving mass
and into the river. For the majority of these
the attempt is futile.
They try to work from pool to pool
over the rocks where the water is shallowest.
Those who succeed must head into the torrents
of the canyons, where the expected stopping places
are gone. The leaps the salmon repeatedly initiate
up the cataracts

are beyond their endurance. The exhausted fish
are driven downstream.
A few spawn uselessly
along the banks of the lower river
before death.

But always that galaxy of salmon
turns and turns offshore in the salt sky
as if out of the swirling rotation
a thought will take shape and
flash along the neurons,
some action to ensure their survival,
a plan
not yet formed.

THE RUNNERS

As I strolled the seawall
in the rain, clouds low
above the inlet,
three men jogged past me with such an effortless stride
I suddenly took up their pace
behind them. I don't think they
were a lot younger than me
or older, but they stepped easily
through the downpour,
large-bodied, talking in a friendly manner
to each other. They didn't seem to mind
me joining them, called back
greetings and a few questions
about the weather
as we pounded along, skirting puddles
and dodging umbrellaed walkers
on the path. I knew I was in no shape
for this, but remembered people's opinions
that mine are runner's legs, and continued
—yet saved my breath rather than
say much to the others.
I had no idea
where we were running,
they with their wide shoulders
and confident stride,
but I felt no matter what obstacles
or quest we faced
if anyone could win
it was men like these.
Or maybe we were running for nothing
splashing through the afternoon rain
only to run. And soon I
was too busy keeping my body with them
to care about where we were going.

A YELLOW COTTAGE

1

Transparent waves
Of the lake
Slap
Onto stones and sand
Steps of planks and earth
Lead up a steep bank

To a yellow cottage
One of many dwellings
That line this
Summer bay
From here
The miles of water
Reach Long Duck Island
Then wooded shores
Without houses, except
The tiny dock
Of a monastery
Then
Other islands

To the north end, where a creek
Winds back from a cove, among marshes
And stands of maple and birch to
The first in a chain
Of empty lakes
Dirt roads
Swing south once more
Or stop
As the water retraces a path
Through distant mountains
To the edge of
The icy sea

2

A flat stone
Taken up from the beach

Held
Like this

And spun
Toward the sun-sparkling lake

An adult's hand
Propelling the stone

So it bounces
Once, twice, more

On the shimmering
Water

While a child's fingers
Scratch amid pebbles

Grasp another stone
Fling it down into clear waves

No, this way
Again the adult hand

Skips a stone
Circle to circle

That hand then shows hands
How to choose

How to hold
To throw

And the child's toss this
Time

      Strikes
And lifts

      Soars
The stone suspended

The child's fingers

Lengthening, becoming graceful

In the bright air

3

Up at the cottage
Sounds of the birds, faint boat engines
The voices of children
From a neighbor's
Or along the lane

Trees around the house
Rustle

Their foliage
A shifting pattern
Of shadow
On a yellow wall

On the wood porch floor

A white wall
Indoors, beside a window

4

Under this August sun
A woman
Is dying

Neither very young nor old, she waits
Below the noisy leaves
Watching her children play

Where she played
Much has changed, nothing
Has changed

Her parents
Still spend the hot days
Swimming, canoeing

With children, now
Grandchildren

Across the lane
In Yelle's field
Grasshoppers

Leap through the tall hay

Grasshoppers to be caught
Cupped
In an adult's hand, a child's

Hand
And let free

5

One morning
She picks up a pail
For berries
And goes out the cottage door

She hugs each
of her two young daughters, they
Demand to go with her
As before, but she

With her sad
Beautiful face
Sighs and

Kisses them
She embraces her husband
Her parents
Sisters, brother, friends

And starts to walk
Through the fields
Toward the hill

Where berries
Grow: straw-
Berries on the upland meadows
Raspberries higher in the tangled brush

As she has loved to
Girl and woman
She wants to gather, to eat while picking
And bring home

She climbs
And sees beyond a wood on the near shore
The blue cloud of the lake
And the far Laurentians
At last, in a favorite spot
She reaches to touch
The red fruit amid
The green thorns
Placing one berry
In her mouth to
Savor
The sudden pure
Delight, she sets to work
To provide
This joy again
For the others down the hill
For all her world

Until her fingers
Discover on a stem
A pulpy
Discolored hybrid
She holds for a moment
A dark
Lump
She brings to her lips

6

Lake water
Cools the body when immersed
In the heat of day
Or warms it
After dark

In a boat's shadow
Reeds and mud are visible
On the bottom

Minnows school
Above stones or
Furrows of sand

7

Lake air
Brings light
To the veins of the leaves
To nourish
And consume

Over this rocky shore

Where a spirit
Has left the earth

And remains

from
THE ASTONISHING WEIGHT
OF THE DEAD
(1994)

WOMAN WHO CALLS HORSES

On a Valley road, I saw
through the dusk, a figure in a white dress
hovering in a field whose green
had nearly all been drained.
She stared past a deep gully
toward a far part of the pasture
where it seemed white horses grazed.
And I heard her
whinny,
the sound carried to me
above the steady thin grinding
of crickets
under a half moon. As I watched
she whinnied again,
raising and lowering her outstretched arms
but nothing happened.
                    And then the faintest
tremor in the earth
like distant thunder
growling, then hoofbeats,
then out of the night
the spectral face
of a white horse running,
then another, five in all
closing the distance toward her
as she ran back toward the fence
then turned, standing her ground,
the horses cantering to a stop
churning around her, hoofs and manes,
her white clothes,
their white hair,
her hand now on one's nose
now another's flank,
as they shifted and jostled

surrounding her
                until one
spun about
and began trotting
back to the darkness
and then a second, then
the small herd was receding, galloping
into sound
and then only the crickets' drone.

And I heard
the woman laugh, a wild
night laugh
of fierceness
and pleasure
and dread

THE MAN WHO LOGGED THE WEST RIDGE

The man who logged the West Ridge,
unlike the person who owns it,
has his home on the Valley floor.
The money this man got
for taking away the West Ridge's trees
paid a crew, made payments on a truck
and a skidder, reduced a mortgage, bought food
and a new outboard
and was mailed off to the owner.

So the fir and larch and pine
of the Ridge, its deer and coyote,
snails and hummingbirds,
were dollars for a brief time,
then were gone from our Valley.
Fair enough. While the logging was in progress
the man stood on the new road along the slope
to shout at a pickup full of people from below
over the howls of the saws
and the surging diesels:
I don't have to talk to you.
I am leaving a few trees. I don't have to do that.
Bug me, and I'll level this place completely.

Once the West Ridge was empty,
the owner put the land up for sale.
Remaining that close to the sky
is slash, and the churned soil,
heaps of cable and plastic oil containers
and a magazine of photographs
of young women's breasts and vaginas
that got passed around one lunchhour
and looked at, while everyone ate their sandwiches
resting against some logs. Nobody wanted to keep
the publication, not even the one who brought it,
so its pages lie on the earth near a torn-out stump,
the paper shrivelling into rain.

And the man who logged the Ridge
is finished with it, although he and the rest of us
constantly traverse its lowest levels
where the lane winds between our houses
and fields
toward the highway. Yet the Ridge
is not finished with the Valley
—its shadow continues to slip down its creekbeds
every afternoon
darkening the land as far as the river
while the other side still receives the sun.
That shadow, once of a forest,
now is born from an absence, from money,
from eight weeks' work.
We live each day shadowed by the Ridge,
neighbors of the man who cut it down.

COUNTRY PLEASURES

When I wake in the morning
I can tell by the frost on my beard
and the blanket
that both the electricity and the fire are out again.
I stagger into the washroom
but nothing comes from the taps
except a macabre rattle and gasp:
water line must have frozen solid
just like this time last year.
I'm about to descend to the basement
to see if I can rekindle the furnace at least
when the noise of an unusual commotion distracts me.
At first I think a bird or two
has fallen down the chimney once more
or perhaps the colony of wasps
who have settled in my outer walls
have decided to swarm. Yet when I follow the sound
to its source
I see to my horror a wounded deer chased by some dogs
has chosen my porch to die on.
I yank open the door and the dogs run away
but the deer, its sides heaving,
is pretty badly chewed up.
My rifle is of course at Norm's, the gunsmith,
for repairs
and those of my neighbors who aren't militant vegetarians
are on the other side than me of a bitter dispute
over a proposed clearcut of half the community watershed.
I reach for the phone,
meaning to inform the government Fish and Wildlife Branch
about the deer,
but find the two-year-old with whom I share my party line
has already begun his daily self-discovery
of telecommunication skills.

After some minutes of alternately wheedling
and commanding
her or him or it
to hang up the goddam phone so I can call for help
I discard this idea
and attempt to remember where I put the car keys.
I step onto my deck
walking around the apparently-comatose deer
who nevertheless opens its eyes as I pass
giving forth a piteous groan.
The car, only fifteen or twenty tries later, surges into life
and after checking both directions down the not-yet-plowed road
I head out toward the highway
and town.

COUNTRY SOLITUDE

"Living alone out here—
how's your mental health?"
a visiting friend inquired over coffee
with a grin. "Started talking to yourself
yet?"
            Those are good questions,
I replied thoughtfully.
Just a minute and I'll check.
My friend's glance was quizzical
yet in fact I had been meaning to do
a little self-evaluation.
Listen up, everybody,
I announced. *You know the issue.*
Are we in the pink of emotional fitness
or what? A few voices
began to speak at once
and I observed my friend staring at me,
his mouth slightly open.
One at a time, one at a time,
I admonished. But the results I was getting
were mixed.
Okay, let's take a straw poll,
I decreed. The eyes of my friend
were flicking anxiously between me
and the door. *Quick,* I continued.
Those who think we're functioning well
put up your hands. Right.
Now, all who believe we might
have gone a bit off the rails
lift your *hands.*
My friend had risen from his chair.
I did a rapid addition.
Some of you aren't voting,
I noted sternly. *Let's try it again.*

My friend was fumbling at his jacket,
his lips pursed
as if silently whistling.
Yet the outcome of the vote was clear.
You don't have to worry about me
spending this time by myself,
I said in the direction of my friend's back
while he struggled with the doorknob.
We're doing fine.

THE POLITICS OF THE HOUSE: TABLES

Tables are egalitarians.
Each stands on its four legs
and whatever is placed on them—a sumptuous cloth
and silver cutlery
or a paper cover with plastic plates and spoons—
the table knows its purpose is the same.
Even the most exquisitely carved sort
are cautioned by their parents when young:
Never forget: take our chairs away from us
and all we are is a shelf.
But as long as we bear up
those objects we are asked to hold
we are each successfully doing our work in the world.

In this way tables are like horses:
indifferent to whether they carry a rich man
on an expensive saddle
or a young girl bareback, pull a plough
or a carriage of tourists. Certain kinds of horses
are best for specific jobs
but among horses themselves there are no hierarchies.
A Clydesdale believes itself as accomplished in its own way
as an Arabian, neither one deferring to
nor lording it over the other.

Unlike horses, though,
tables remain a sign of human civilization:
a central item of our houses—kitchen table,
sewing table—and our cities
—workbench, packing table.
Sadly, the men and women around the boardroom table
still imagine themselves worth more
than the women and men seated at the lunchroom tables

on their break. Yet in the midst
of all our ranking and gradations,
qualifications, certificates, and ornate hats,
tables
patiently continue to demonstrate
the ubiquitous nature of equality.

THE POLITICS OF THE HOUSE: CHAIRS

Any chair is a success
if it can support a woman or man

without collapsing.
Chairs may be padded, or bare, shaped wood,

foldable, stackable
or reclining. Yet each

in its prime is our ally:
who isn't thankful for

an opportunity to sit down?
Of course there are renegade chairs—

hard and uncomfortable
making a meeting, lecture

or even a dinner party
unendurable.

Also, there are office chairs
designed to be below the height

of one other person's chair in a room
to intimidate us,

to teach us what the owner of these chairs
thinks is our place.

Yet outlaw chairs
are the exception,

are in no way representative
of chairdom. Chairs are the essence

of what befriends us on this planet.
We travel greater distances in chairs,

for instance, than on beds
or even our own feet.

And although many of the tasks
we have to do to keep the world going

are performed standing up,
an enormous number get accomplished

while we are seated.
And other jobs could be:

after years of doctors trying to force us
to give birth on our backs, for example,

we have begun to return
to a more natural position—

using a birthing stool, the chair
of life. In fact, chairs adopt the attitude

of the Earth toward humanity:
ever-present, neutral toward our individual achievements

but generally hospitable
to the endeavors of our species.

For these reasons
it is easy to comprehend why

some primitive tribes buried their dead
in a sitting position.

After all, if there is a life beyond this one,
probably in that existence, too,

more will have to be done seated
than stretched out—loafing or sleeping.

What does seem mysterious
is why none of these early peoples

developed a burial chair.
Such an object obviously would represent

a veneration owed the most useful human construct.
No doubt such artifacts are absent

because unlike weapons, pottery, jewelry
or anything else found in ancient graves

chairs are too valuable
to mail on to the next world.

THE POLITICS OF THE HOUSE: ALARM CLOCK

As soon as you are old enough
you are given or must buy
the smallest, most portable part
of a school, a factory,
or every place where
you are summoned, dismissed and otherwise given orders
with whistles and horns.

The rulers of these institutions
make it a requirement that you keep
this thermostat of the hours,
this mandatory tool
near at hand
and especially in the room where you are closest
to escaping their control:
where you stretch out
     make love
         dream

Long before electronic pagers
the alarm clock
linked us continually
to whoever bought and sold our time.
Like some household shrine
this instrument
receives our devotions twice daily during the workweek
—once when we shut if off, and again
when we set it.
Even on holidays
its presence reminds us of a power
greater than our wishes.
This is the sole domestic appliance
we each consider necessary to possess
yet regard with loathing.

I believe this device
constantly reveals
a sickness at the core of our lives:
what kind of social structure
needs these mechanical or electric cattle prods
in every house
in order to function?
Is no other way possible
to arrange the work of the world
without forcing us to board at our home
this pitiless timekeeper
        this company stooge
                this factory foreman
                from a century before?

CORRECTING 120 ESSAYS ON POETRY

My task is dry
as brittle paper
the red pencil
scratching scratching
—sand
caught between metal parts
forced to slide
open/shut

Sometimes what they have created
is strangely
beautiful:
a wooden sculpture
almost spherical
half the size
of a basketball
I run my palms and fingers
around and around it
notice a rough part
write: *awkward; could be smoother*
at this spot
Later they read my comment
Their eyes say
I know that

Or
what they hand in
is shaped in a rush
or crude
grotesque
because they were absent
or inattentive
when the directions were given
they did not know
were thinking of other problems, joys

I examine each of these constructs
just as gravely as the others
rotating them before me
on the desk
Such creations seem
a rejected version
a piece
left with the shavings and wood chips
under a workbench
after a false start
or dropped by mistake
My hands travel
across the surface
find a deep furrow
gouged
I write *you have a furrow*
here
But when the makers
hold again what they devised
they do not read
any words: their eyes
seek the letter
or number I attach
to this broken thing
When they read that
they nod
toss the malformed object
away

DID I MISS ANYTHING?

Question frequently asked by
students after missing a class

Nothing. When we realized you weren't here
we sat with our hands folded on our desks
in silence, for the full two hours

> Everything. I gave an exam worth
> 40 per cent of the grade for this term
> and assigned some reading due today
> on which I'm about to hand out a quiz
> worth 50 per cent

Nothing. None of the content of this course
has value or meaning
Take as many days off as you like:
any activities we undertake as a class
I assure you will not matter either to you or me
and are without purpose

> Everything. A few minutes after we began last time
> a shaft of light descended and an angel
> or other heavenly being appeared
> and revealed to us what each woman or man must do
> to attain divine wisdom in this life and
> the hereafter
> This is the last time the class will meet
> before we disperse to bring this good news to all people on earth

Nothing. When you are not present
how could something significant occur?

> Everything. Contained in this classroom
> is a microcosm of human existence
> assembled for you to query and examine and ponder
> This is not the only place such an opportunity has been gathered
>
> but it was one place
>
> And you weren't here

FIRST-YEAR ENGLISH FINAL

These seem papers
singed by fire
—documents left scattered
in a hectic retreat of
battalion headquarters
or the abandoned records
of an overthrown regime

Fear and pain
shimmer over the disorganized pages
hover above the words scratched along the slots
lined onto the white surface

And rage
flares in the ink
deposited frantically here
It is anger that matches my own
knuckle to knuckle
as I read the words
as my red pen
descends toward its victims
toward what is written
Once more
I have failed
to convince, to inform
to teach

> So I hold their fury
> stacks of it
> sheets of it
> and press down on theirs
> with my own

> > How did literature
> > become so filled
> > with hate?

Document your sources correctly
the red nib admonishes
You must provide examples
to show *what you mean*

The blue paragraphs
howl
WE DID NOT ASK TO DO THIS

No one is listening

SURE, I WAS PAID WELL

but the money felt
like a thick stack of bills
had been folded once and crammed in my open mouth

so what I wanted to say
was blocked, or at the very least garbled
by the wad of dollars

                        and my jaws ached
with the strain of being held apart
by the cash. Though I tried to dress well

I wasn't sure if people on the street
mocked me behind my back
for being so funny-looking

with a mouth stuffed with currency.
Or maybe they didn't see me at all
but only saw the clump of bills

that pressed down on my tongue.
When I sought out others paid as much as me
I found myself calculating how thick

their gag of dollars was
compared to mine. In any case
it was difficult to talk about the experience we had in common

since their words were hard to distinguish
through the money. And I confess
I was afraid to stick my fingers in behind

and lever the currency out; I was fearful of
what was dammed up
behind that cash,

of what the absence of those dollars
would release. And I was anxious
that the wad of money

would turn out to be an illusion:
a few genuine bills on the outside of the roll
and the rest only paper,

paper.

GETTING THE NEWS

At her words, the small boy inside me
is shoved face forward
trips, hits gravel
and begins to slide
Pebbles tear open
palms and knees
peeling the flesh back
like flames shrivelling paper
Grains of rock embed themselves
in the expanding cuts
so when I coast to a stop
in a blur of pain
and stand shakily erect
I attempt only once to brush clear
skinned flesh:
my blunt hands
force gravel further into my wounds
Alone on the road
my hurts filming over with blood
I swallow air
ready to howl my agony
swallow air
air

RETURN TO THE HEART

The sound of the river had not changed:
the glacial torrent cutting between
black rock piled on rock
scattered down this valley one season
when water poured over the mountain barrier.
I crouched to drink
in the midst of the icy spray
and the throbbing
of the river pushing among these stones.

Where the stream widens
to form an island of
alder and cottonwood
the water is fast, but not deep
and it is possible to cross
cautiously balancing from rock to rock.
Twenty-five years ago
I came alone once to this place
a boy near the edge of adulthood
carrying my heart.

Or is this not
memory, but a dream
or reverie? Yet I recall
how for most of a morning
I built a structure of poles and stones.
I took a small bag from my pack
and mixed concrete at the pebbled edge of the island
then took my heart
and set it
at the centre of what I had constructed
and sealed it in
and turned away.

> I had decided I did not need
> whatever uses the organ served.

For years after, I worked at my life.
I had what I thought were good friends
and lovers, walked in fire
and deep cold, laughed much and
felt sharp pain.

But in the cavity in my chest
where the heart was absent
a fluid unknown to medicine
began to collect. At the start the liquid seemed benign
a sort of protective secretion
but after more than two decades
the fluid
shifts
throwing me off balance
when I bend too abruptly toward or
back from another person. Also the liquid
has become acidic
searing the tissue that contains it.

When I described my symptoms
my doctors made notes
and referred me to other physicians.
At last, though, I remembered
my heart.

So I have returned to this wood
with a new pack on my shoulders
and with sledge hammer and shovel.
After the hike in from the old road
I located the island
more densely treed now.
I left my gear on the beach where I crossed
and began to search for
a small mound of cement.

For hours I dodged branches
forcing my way amid the alder trunks and bushes.
Sometimes I crawled across a likely spot

125

feeling with my hand through high grass
or scrabbling amid roots and stones.
At lunchtime, I found a clearing in the undergrowth
and retrieved my pack and equipment
and sat to eat
watching birds and a squirrel in the leaves above me
and the play of light
where the river leapt and fell back.
Near the finish of my meal
I reached to place the cup of my thermos
on a rocky outcrop
and was aware that under moss
this was my heart's grave.

My hands began to shake.
What would be left of my heart
after this long in the dark:
a crumble of dust, or
a desiccated leather bag
or could the organ be
somehow undamaged
by its stay within an airtight space
far from blood and breath?

I scrape off moss
baring grey concrete
and heft the sledge.
Each time the head falls
it bounces once
on the surface
and subsides. I lift my arms
over my right shoulder
and smash the sledge down.
In my ears
is the deafening ring
of steel on stone.

THE HEART IS ALSO A MEADOW

The heart is also
a mountain meadow
a tangle thigh-deep of
hay, ferns
purple thistle
Indian paintbrush
the intense minuscule blue
of forget-me-not
tall angelica along a creekbed
and white-and-brown daisies
scattered everyplace
but especially where years ago
a dirt road curved through

Much could be hidden
in this foliage:
a grouse nest
with five eggs
a sudden charge by the grouse herself
or a bear
that rises out of grass
a few metres away
as if a troop of mounted warriors from another age
lifted up on their horses
weapons and tackle jangling
in the still air

Deer
thread across the meadow
by moonlight

while from a nest aloft
in the brain-stem tree
five ravens
watch

and cry out

Near one edge of this clearing
a cabin
of planks and steeply angled tin roof
stands
None of the ordinary litter
of human habitation
surrounds it
There is only the grass
and then abruptly
this dwelling
It could be the home
of a witch
or hermit—
the door is sealed
with a rusty padlock
Yet the structure
is in good repair
its windows shuttered
from within
awaiting the return of
whatever once
lived here

MODIFICATIONS TO THE HEART

In a child, the heart is plump
but strong with the tenseness
of young limbs.
Occasionally, though, an event
will tear open the covering of the organ
like a knee scraped bloody in a spill from a bicycle.
The wound is painful for days,
then heals completely.

Yet insecurities
or a hideous incident or situation
involving the boy or girl
can grip the heart
and twist it
to a barely recognizable shape.
Thus the modification of the heart
may commence early—the organ might or might not
ever recover its whole function.

And for each person there awaits a first
betrayal or loss
usually experienced in adolescence
that permanently marks the heart,
even if the only evidence years later
is a slight nick or scar.
Thereafter, the blows begin to strike
with increasing rapidity
in the normal course of adult love
and rejection.
Mostly these assaults
result in bruises and other surface discoloration
that disappear in time
but underlying tissue also can be injured.
The latter damage, as with some childhood hurt
that weakened subsurface muscle and fibres,

might be undetected for years
until a portion of the heart one Thursday after a meal
collapses.

And from time to time, a wound is inflicted so deeply
—either in a single moment
with a sharp blow like a knife's
or in a jagged tear
ripped slowly apart during weeks or months
of excruciating pain—
that medical intervention is required.
This can take the form of stitches
or a metal or plastic plate must be implanted
to hold the heart together.
Or, tissue from the brain
or lungs or stomach
must be grafted across the cut.

More ordinary disappointments,
confrontations
and setbacks
also affect the heart:
the thousands of daily jabs
of electrical or adrenalin shock
leave areas of each atrium and ventricle
pockmarked or excessively spongy,
tenderer than usual
or abnormally thickened and coarse.

Such changes to the heart are clearly evident
by a person's forties.
It is common for a man or woman in that decade
to remove the heart
and examine it, noting the differences
from when he or she was younger
and attempting to account for the obvious devastation.
The battered heart sits on a cloth
in front of them, its convoluted surface a morass

of healed and half-healed
notches, slits
and contusions.
Sections of it may have gone dead
from stress or trauma,
other parts are engorged with blood
because of too-active capillaries.
Yet as the owner of the heart watches,
the organ effortlessly
contracts and
expands, apparently capable of absorbing
more
adverse treatment—
of continuing to sustain
a human life.

THE LOVES OF THE PENIS

The penis is blind, and
nods through its ordinary hours
feeling like a drain spout,
an appendix, a mouth
with only one thing to say.
No wonder whenever, due to circumstances
out of its control,
blood suddenly rushes to it
as though messengers are bringing vital news
to a person of importance,
the penis perks right up.
Sightless or not, it rears its head
like a business executive or captain
inspecting what he rules.
However, as with individuals who have spent
much time alone,
the penis is susceptible to such attention
and to flattery. Also, like everything blind
it has a developed sense of touch
and responds inappropriately to
affectionate gestures that involve
even slight physical contact.

In gratitude for any notice,
for being singled out,
the penis falls in love too easily
—like a puppy eager to please,
eager for a home.
As might be expected
of someone who not only cannot see
but is emotionally vulnerable, the penis
is not very discriminating
about its amours.
Even experience
appears to teach it nothing.

After a period of solitude
or unhappiness
it loses nearly all sense of judgement.
Like an addict, or anybody who depends
on external stimulus for
self-validation, it forgets
the unpleasant consequences
of its previous compulsive behaviors
and leaps at the chance
once more, for love.

THE WINLAW ELEGIES

Winlaw, in heavy rain
Down country roads, the May leaves
have burst out on stems and branches
In a flower bed, below early tulips
the blade of a gladiolus
breaks the surface
like the dorsal fin of a shark

This past twelvemonth, the earth received
more of my dead
From the moment they were born, this is the only Spring
they have not seen
—along the lane, the hillsides
choked with alder
and the underbrush's puffs of blossoms
floating through the steadily falling water

The trees, weeds, grass stalks
push out of the soaked ground
with as much haste as they can
as though they shared our species' repugnance
for lying still, covered with soil
Each green flag is an affirmation, a cry of joy
long live the living
Each a perfect elegy
for what remains in the damp dark
for what goes under
and does not return

MOUNTAIN ELEGY

Dave Bostock

Late on the day of his death,
high in the alpine
above the trees, I crossed a field
more stone than earth
and found what I had climbed for.
Where ice and the cold
pummel the hard ground,
where frost and the relentless glacial wind
tear at whatever tries to live,
the moss campion
adheres to bits of soil
lichens have generated over eons
from rock. The campion, too,
has infinite patience:
a decade passes
before it will flower.
After a quarter-century
it spreads no wider
than the outstretched fingers of a hand.
But the flower digs in, buffeted by the nightly chill,
by solar rays, by hail, the Spring melt,
smothered for much of the year beneath snow.
Air trapped in its leaves
and clusters, however,
forms a minute protected place
out of the wind and
warmed by sun.
Here, other plants are born
and nurtured.

                His laughter
                was such an enclosure
                in the roaring life below.
                One time I'd been working welding
                on a logging show in the Charlottes

I had a couple of grand saved
so decided to quit. This was when
if you had any kind of trade, any kind of ticket
you were in demand.
It was no big deal to change jobs.
On Friday
I picked up my pay, and made a point
of finding the boss
and telling him exactly, in detail,
what I thought of him
and where he could put
the whole outfit. Then I was on the plane
for Rupert, with some of the other guys.
We'd already had plenty to drink
before we even got on board.

On Monday I woke up
in the Rupert Hotel.
I had no idea
how I had spent the weekend
but I discovered I was absolutely broke.
Every cent of my two thousand dollars was gone.
I phoned to the camp I just left
and asked if I could have my job back.
"Sure, Dave," the boss said.
"Report as soon as you get in."
"Uh, Mr. Johnson?" I had to say.
"Could you advance me the money
for the plane? I don't have
quite enough to cover the fare."
"Okay," he said. That's how it was at the time:
tear a strip off 'em on Friday
and grovel on Monday
and they'd rehire you.
It was special. Try that today, though,
and see how far you get.

I camped that night
just above treeline, by a cluster of dwarf firs,

a *krumholz*, formed on the barren
by a single plant
whose roots tunnel upslope
and emerge, or whose branches
pushed down by snow
take root. Such gatherings, too,
create within themselves
an eddy of more hospitable weather
in the high, harsh air.
These conifer islands are also how trees advance,
pushing toward the summit: forerunners
marking and clearing a path
others will follow in relative certainty
and ease.

> *I had a job with a pile driving crew*
> *—metal piles. The company was Ontario-based*
> *and I think this was the first time*
> *they had hired union labor.*
> *Anyway, one of their foremen*
> *was forever showing up to order you to do*
> *some task you'd already begun.*
> *I'd have finished a weld*
> *and was packing up my gear to move*
> *to the next spot, when the foremen would come by*
> *and say: "Dave, I want you to pack your equipment*
> *and haul it over there for the next weld."*
> *For a time this guy only seemed silly*
> *but one morning—I don't know, it was a bad day*
> *or something—he really started to bother me.*
> *When for the nine-hundredth time*
> *the foreman ordered me to start*
> *what I already was in the middle of,*
> *I lost it. I began to whine, real loud:*
> *"Aww, you're always telling me*
> *to do that. I don't wanna. Why do I*
> *have to go down in that hole*
> *and weld? How come you don't tell*
> *anybody else to do it?"*

The foreman's face went white.
He didn't know what to say.
He backed off, but others on the crew had heard
and a few minutes later I heard a whine
from over by the crane:
"I don't wanna do that. You're always
saying I have to. How come I
have to be the one to do it?"
After this, there was no stopping the guys.
All over the site, whenever the foreman
tried to tell anybody anything
you'd hear this incredible whining:
"Awww. I don't wanna." Afterwards, we called it
a whine-in. The foreman
only lasted a couple more days
then he was gone.

The heat of my fire
slashes at my face
when I bend to lever
a log further into the flames.
The song of his life—his work,
his music, his joy—
brought him a cancer that spread
through his body, shrunken
beyond remedy, and then the pneumonia
he chose
to let kill him.
From the peaks around me in the dark,
wind and sun and the earth's turning
bring the snowpack
to the valleys we dwell in
—whether as water
or cold air
we breathe, and then we don't breathe,
leaving behind
our laughter or rage,
our unfinished stories
whispered toward the stars.

THE ASTONISHING WEIGHT OF THE DEAD

I am amazed
by the heaviness of the dead.
Whenever a dozen or so
of my dead are
seated around my front room
the cushions of the sofa and chairs
sink
under them, as if they lived.
These gatherings
like a small party
bring together those previously acquainted
and those from very distant
parts of my life.
At the first of these occasions
I was nervous some wouldn't get along.
But although death has preserved
the shape and gestures of their bodies
as well as the core of their
personalities, all seemed in a mood
to be amiable.
At the start, however, I tried anxiously
to keep conversation flowing,
to introduce Dave, for example, with his wonderful stories
to Joan, of the bright humorous eyes.
Where I saw two aunts from opposite sides of the family
who vaguely knew each other
chatting, I made a point of drawing in
Henrietta, who was about their age
and who I felt they'd enjoy.
But my twitching from group to group
was not needed—a hum of measured talk
rose from everyplace
along with laughter.
All were speaking pleasantly together
and at times one would rise

and cross the room to attach herself or himself
to a different twosome or threesome.
No one subservient
or boasting, each expressing in word and posture
the quiet confidence of
the vanished, present at my house
of an evening.
And the carpet
in its pile the next day
carries the imprint of their passages
and where they sat
or sprawled:
testimony
to the weight
of the astonishing dead.

WALEY, WALEY

The boat will drift the last distance
to the dock
and I will climb out
and smell again
the pine forest along this side of the river
and the sweet woodsmoke
of the village chimneys.
At the front of the small crowd
waiting for me
is my wife, my bride,
with my young son in her arms
and Rachel, my daughter, peering
from behind her.
Then we are embracing,
and me awkward with the boy,
he squirming, Rachel shy, withdrawing.
But my friends
press around us
shouts of joy,
and laughter.
There are many present I thought
I would never greet again
—Dennis, with a witty quip
I only half hear, but no mistaking
his hug, Dave joking as before,
"Glad to meet you,
partner," handshake,
others, too, everyone excited with
bits of conversation
crossing and being misunderstood
and corrected with hilarity
and inquiries after missing friends.
Then we are all walking
the street, the log and plank houses
of the village
little changed from my memory of them,

people I don't know coming to doors and windows
to watch us pass, calling out,
members in our group bantering back,
laughing, Dennis says: "It's almost a parade."
"A procession!"
a voice at the rear cries.
And she walking beside me
her hand in mine, the flesh
soft and tight and familiar.
We enter the yard
of the rough wood synagogue
where the rabbi has come to the porch door
to receive us. I stand a pace or two from the others
alone before him
for his blessing,
his lined face hardly aged
as he leads the prayers.
Something tugs at my fingers:
Rachel has darted forward
to seize my hand, watching the ground
but holding fast. The small crowd thins
when we turn back to the street,
dispersing into the smoky evening
with promises to meet tomorrow.
The four of us
my family
journey a little further to the old house
and enter.

She moves through the rooms
arranging supper
and settling the children
while I watch: amazed to be once more
inside these walls, under these roof beams,
crossing these wood floors.
She shows me the newest
domestic changes: cloth she has woven
for the table, a new bench
by a window. And the latest

domestic problems: a sticking door latch,
where water is seeping around a fixture.
As of old, I begin to plan
how to tackle these,
the steady decay and resurrection of this house,
of any house, a rhythm I did not know I missed.
And then the meal, and the baby to bed,
and going in with her to Rachel,
and Rachel asking,
when I bend to kiss her,
"Will you be here in the morning?"
And I say: "Every morning. Now."
And Rachel turning over drowsily
under her covers.
Then seeing to the house lights,
suddenly awkward with each other,
the bedspread aglow in the last soft flame.

I waken deep in the blackness
and lie listening to the silences
of the house, its breathing
and creaks.
As carefully as possible
I swing my legs out
and stand naked in the room.
I move to the window
and shift the curtain,
looking out at the ridge
that rises to the west behind us,
its trees darker shapes
in darkness.
It is very late
yet I notice a light where Larry, the closest neighbor,
has come outside to shiver at the stars.
Perhaps the opening of the curtain
caught his eye: his face, lit by his open door,
swings to face this house, and he waves,
waves a welcome.
He points upwards, to remind me, perhaps,

of his old habit of checking the stars,
then he shrugs and goes in. The hour, the river beyond
the village, the forested mountain
are mine.

When I turn from the window,
her eyes, bright with love,
are watching me. We smile at each other.
A moment later I will be back in bed,
sharing a final kiss
before sinking into the warm
eternal
night.

NEW POEMS

FOR WILLIAM STAFFORD (1914–1993)

Travelling in the dusk, I hit a deer
on the Monashee Highway west of the Needles ferry

A brown blur
passed above the hood

then the metallic gasp and
thud of two vehicles that collide

The truck drove on
all the dashboard gauges normal

while I steered to the shoulder
and braked, the motor idling

On either side, forested mountains
bore their silent February snows

I rounded the front of the truck
and stopped: it had been caved in

as though I had struck a post
—the bumper bent outwards

to a semicircle, grill smashed
piercing the radiator, coolant leaking down

in weak streams
One headlight shone ahead

but the other was wrenched 90 degrees
through shattered glass

I mounted again
and swung the engine's final minutes

across the asphalt and back
to see the deer

which lay facing east
dead

one eye aimed toward me
like a rifle

or a gold coin burnished to a flash
or the illumination device

of a vessel
from a different sun

THE QUARREL

They had been out
getting firewood.
She thought going as a family
would be good: the children
could have a day
outdoors with their Dad. He
wanted to go with Rob,
his friend, in Rob's pickup
like the two of them did
almost every year,
but after the quarrel
about how could he stack logs
in a goddamn station wagon
full of kids, and she pointed out
without getting mad
they could use the trailer
he hauled the skidoo in,
he finally agreed
it was An Okay Idea.
But now he's pissed off
because you have to watch
those two kids every goddamn minute
so everything takes five times as long,
but mostly because
the chain saw choked and died
and he couldn't restart it
after trying six hundred times
and so the trailer is only half full
which means he'll have to come back again
by himself, since Rob went last weekend
knowing he was going to go this Sunday
with the goddamn Family,
and because now this completely worthless
piece of useless shit
of a car isn't starting either
and here they are up the back of beyond

and didn't he say you just don't take kids
cutting firewood
that it's not like a visit to a
stupid waterslide or something?

And he's walking up the logging road
to cool off, thinking
there's something wrong
with this, I shouldn't
be married
to her
And she's sitting alone in the
front seat, reassuring the children
in back,
telling herself *there's something wrong with*
me,
why aren't I
happy? I know he isn't perfect
but we're married
and every other couple we know
may have their troubles but
the wives seem content

And by March
she will have been living in a one-bedroom
motel suite, with the kids,
three months
although she tells her friends
it isn't as bad
as it seems:
the children could stay in the same
school
and one of their classmates even lives
at the motel,
and sooner or later some place
will come up she can afford
and it's not like
this is forever

POST-SECONDARY EDUCATION

The moon appeared in the dark lake
the moment it crested the hills.

In my car speeding north, the student
I had given a lift to

said: "The old guys
should get out of our way." He meant

musicians, writers, politicians
—our conversation had shifted to the roots

of the present. "The aged need to step aside,
make room for the young."

The highway was four lanes
but not much traffic so late. The moon

had climbed above the eastern ridge now.
I didn't say

Perhaps the people you mention
waited years

to achieve their status.
What if they intend to savor

where they are? Should they disappear
because you're as impatient

as they were once?
And I didn't say

Look at the full moon
racing us up the lake.

I didn't say
How beautiful the moon is

high over the valley rim.
I held onto the wheel

and I drove.

WHERE MOUNTAIN WATER

Where mountain water
rolls stone down from the screes
I knelt
in an alder wood
on an island in that torrent

Around me lay the hammer and crowbar
I had used to break
concrete poured a quarter-century ago
when I had sealed away
my heart

Now through the crumbled cement
I glimpsed pale blue
Carefully I chiselled at rubble
A rich, sour, earthy odor
as of hay
rose from the shrivelled sack
when I eased it
into open air

I held my heart
bloodless, its ghastly bluish tinge
streaked with dirt
and white dust
Its sides felt like
thin pliable cardboard
in my fingers

and I grieved

for all the heart
might have taught me
for what the heart I did not know
could have spoken to women and men
—table-words, bed-words, desk-words

words at the microphone
and by myself in the street
I grieved for the loneliness
of the gap where my heart was absent
and how I have given that lack
to every person
close to me
I grieved kitchens
without butter, a porch
without geraniums, rugs without
candles, roads
with pre-recorded songs

I awoke
and saw on the mountainside behind me
a landscape churned empty by machines
just a few snags standing
a single cottonwood at the rim of a draw
skid trails
stacks of branches
and stumps, roots
heaped
to be burned
The chainsaw, the wheel
of the skidder
were in my hands
—two palms that grasped
what long before had been
my heart

I turned
from my pack and tools
and walked toward the creek
I guessed tears
could not irrigate, rejuvenate
But I planned to wedge the exiled organ
among rocks
to learn if the flowing meltwater
would restore it

I am not sure
if I can ever again
merge with my heart
It seems to me only by
prying myself ajar
with horrible pain
can the blood's universe be inserted
into my body once more
Yet if the heart is flooded, whole
perhaps out on the world-ridge
I will encounter someone to advise me
how I might mend
And if not, at least for joy
and penance
I could walk the rest of my life
carrying a full heart

IN A HOUSE OF WOMEN

in a house of
women, i walk
carefully, watch
my feet on the
rugs, my hands
on the chairs

i avoid these women
when i can, as
in the woods
i avoid bears
or trees

in this house
are Crow-woman
and Turtle-woman, Porcupine-
woman and Hummingbird-woman

i recognize their names

but whatever they are, they are not
what i know

just as they
do not know what
they imagine they do

what a man is
for, for example

i hear the women tell each other
they wanted rescue
but the man put them
in a home, to which
he brought back
sperm and money

neither was enough, and
the man also insisted
strict accounts be kept
of each, and the unused portions
returned to him

while he
mostly stayed
in another place

i hear the women say
they and their children
are marooned
when the man did not get
what he wanted
he disappeared, while the woman
who did not earn what she
desired
remains

to responsibly, doggedly
serve
the old
error

in a house of women
a howl
leaps from fingers
settling wildflowers in a blue vase

packages left on counters
hide cosmetics
or poison

outside
the first drops of rain
tap the leaves in the aspen grove
shushing them
for the entrance of
the storm that follows, a frantic downpour

THE ROAD'S SIDE

> "Wayman's closest relationships seem to be
> with highways rather than women."
> —critic John Harris

One evening, Wayman heads out for a drive.
The highway appears pleased to see him,
offering a beautiful curving ascent
like a smooth happy melody
followed by a glide back down like an osprey or raven.
Then the highway seems
to have something on her mind.
Wayman powers through a bend
to encounter warning signs about a flagperson
and a minute later reaches the back of
a lineup of stopped vehicles.
Wayman climbs down from his truck to stretch.
"We need to talk," the highway
informs him. "Ok-ay," Wayman agrees cautiously.
"You know I'm delighted to
spend time with you again," the highway says.
"As a friend, you're wonderful: when you're with me
you give 100 per cent appreciation.
But suddenly you're not available; you're off
doing something else."
"I've been busy,"
Wayman protests: "There's been extra duties at work
and my garden to tend."
"I'm aware these activities are part...,"
the highway states patiently, raising a hand
to deflect Wayman's familiar objection,
"of who you are. But I'm not sure
this situation is what I need.
Do you expect me to simply wait
until you decide to visit?"
"What you want," Wayman proclaims irritably,
"is for me to give up my writing,
my job and my house, and just ride around with you?"

"I didn't say that," the highway responds.
"That's what I hear," Wayman sulks.
"If I'm going to be close to someone
I want him with me," the highway replies.
"I need somebody able to commit.
I value the times I share with you
yet too often you choose to be elsewhere."
"I get the same comment
from women," Wayman protests. "Except they complain
about my being with you."
"They've got a point,"
the highway declares: "My counsellor tells me
a person behaves much the same
in every aspect of their lives. How you treat women
isn't likely to be any different than how you treat me."
From up the line
floats the crescendo of engines starting
and one by one pairs of rear lights
glow redly through the dark.
"We'll have to finish this discussion
later," Wayman says with relief,
opening the truck door.
"There may not be another opportunity,"
the highway announces.
"I don't believe I can go on like this."
"Let's agree to talk soon,"
Wayman proposes desperately,
noting the van only a few cars ahead
has begun to move.
"I really care for you," Wayman asserts,
"and I don't want to lose the connection between us.
I have to motor over to Kelowna on Monday.
We can talk then."
"Right: once more you'll see me when it's convenient
for you, and are unavailable when it's not,"
the highway observes.
Wayman twitches anxiously from one foot to another
as the car in front of him grinds into gear.
"But I guess I have no choice," the highway sighs:

"We'll talk Monday."
"Okay, Monday," Wayman mutters,
springing into the driver's seat
like a kid let out of school.
At the first crossroad he pulls onto the shoulder,
waits until the lineup behind him passes
and then swings the truck around
steering for home.

THE BALD MAN

Some women think constantly
of the bald-headed man

There are stories, rhymes
rituals

And in ordinary hours
the women invite him inside

some shyly, some boldly
to look around

like a contractor
to renovate the kitchen

to replace the wallpaper
or like a mechanic

to solve a problem with the engine
The bald man

sings while he works
Sometimes the melody is

unbearably sweet
as ice cream

sometimes the song is gritty and harsh
—siding scorched by fire

or burnt sugar
If the bald-headed man

likes a woman
(and he likes most women)

he leaves a gift—
usually perfume, seawater

a puddle of floor wax
The gift can be a threat

—a clump of rotted leaves
black and shiny with decay

or even a leech
with a fatal bite

But left behind often
is a basket of puppies

a colt, a stook of marvellous hay
that over nine months

must be spun into gold

INSERTION

When we paused, making love, I returned
down to her aromatic lower mouth
and kissed again the moist opening

Then, desiring more, I placed my head
between her legs
so the top of my body rested

against her vulva
and pushed
She groaned

but said *Yes*
and inch by inch
I eased into her

headfirst
amid terrible cries
and shrieks

Yet she never said *Stop*
Imagine how much love
was shown

by her willingness to suffer this agony
this distention
and cramps

and still to allow
to welcome
this insertion

As the pressure on my skull
eased, and I could feel my shoulders
following, I saw, amazed,

I was in a translucent
cavern, the walls
a luminous pink-orange

like gladiolus petals
with the sun behind them
Now my arms and hands

were within, I could feel
the walls of this compartment
rubbery, slightly damp

like salmon flesh
or an orange anemone
but hot

The sound here
was the double beat/pulse
of her heart

reverberating
in this enclosure
leaving nothing else in my ears but

a faint syllable or two
from outside, and the occasional
muted hiss or gurgle

from her guts
In order to fit
all of myself in

I had to pull my knees
toward my chest
so my toes cleared the opening

which closed behind them
and there I was
safe from the world

I noticed a bulge
to the left of my cheek
where my face touched the wall

and I shifted slightly
which brought the protuberance close to my mouth
and I observed

the mound was like a breast
complete with nipple
so I encircled the end with my lips

and began to suck
and my mind, up to now
turbulent with the adventure

began to hum
the single note
the sole thought

that is intense sensual pleasure
so that after a minute
I could not have said

if I was awake or asleep
or separate in any way
from pure joy

THE BIG O

A poet is allowed to use the interjection O
just once in a lifetime.

—rule for writing

Each time I face the fleshly o-
val, the folded and enfolded entrance
with its hairy cap
I wonder
is this it?
is this the O I am permitted?
The tongue, teeth
my whole mouth
working diligently
delicately
draft after draft after draft
is this sweet flow I suck
the Muses' fount that
rises in the cleft
struck by Pegasus?
When a version works
each breath
I take, release
each tongued syllable
vibrates all Mount Helicon
quake after quake

In another version
the seismic probings
that trigger shock
below ground
cause ripple upon ripple to curl
across the field of her belly
—the tempestuous earth-surf
threatening to swamp
the coracle of the navel

Such moments
bring us closer
every time
to the bel-
          low ringing
the pro-
longed ye-
          ES
and counter to
all laws, the
O the   O the
O

THE CALL

Rain in gusts all day
that slackened a little at dusk
but the night
dripping. I sat
in my room
in the dormitory at the edge of the woods
by the edge of the sea.
As I finished a page
in the glare of my desk lamp,
as my fingers caught the paper's upper right corner
to turn it
I heard a voice
—urgent, but without sound—
Go outside
I glanced through the window
at the drizzle
lit with walkway lights.
Again the voice suffused me:
You must go outside
The tone was uncompromising.
Go out and
across the road   Impatience
vibrated in the words
and a sense I was being drawn
to a purpose: a moment
or presence.

      I stood
uneasy. But I walked downstairs,
through the main doors
and felt the first drops soaking into my shirt
to skin. The voice remained certain:
Across the road
Enter the forest

On the closest shoulder of the highway
I paused.
I peered over at the tangle of underbrush and
evergreens. I saw only
rain.

The voice propelled me forward.
On the other side of the road
I halted that much nearer to the woods,
shivering in the chilled damp of my clothes.
Black sky. Heavy downpour now. Wind in the
cedars' gravely swaying tops.

    What would meet me in the dark?
    Nothing but branches and roots
    and the massive trunks of the trees
    showering me
    with winter rain:
    icy ocean's breath
    calling me *fool*

        Or a tall man
        waiting ahead in a clearing
        —one eye socket horribly scarred,
        a raven walking the wet ground
        at his feet,
        a horse nearby
        cropping grass in the forest's
        deep silence

            Or a fire far off
            that as I approach
            I see is ringed with
            cloaked human shapes
            seated at the hissing flames
            A face—now male, now female—
            lifts in my direction
            as I struggle in the drenched brush
            toward them

I trembled
to guess the unknown I was called to
Because I could not understand in advance
this event
I was afraid

Then the sound was the drops
driven by the gale against the hard
surface of the road
and the leaves.
Behind me, past a lawn, the dormitory
rose through rain like a lighted ship.

I turned
to look at the building's doors, stairs,
my room. I began to
retreat.
Yet the instant I swung away
I knew I had spurned a great summons
or gift,
an enormous
chance.

CLOWN SEQUENCE: THE DEATH OF THE CLOWN

i   a collapsed star

            she radiated gravity

wanting to pull to her
all she lacked:

light
a tattered umbrella

        huge shoes
        time

    a flower to squirt water
    colored discs to juggle

money

ii she thought her audience was faithless
and it was

turning away
from her beckoning arms

        that demanded
        total attention

no crowd could sustain
                for long

        she screeched at them
        at their backs
        she honked her horn

the people left

iii in death, she heard the applause
    of silence

    her nose dulled
    to crimson

    then
    black

CLOWN SEQUENCE: THE BURIAL OF THE CLOWN

There was no funeral.
At the cemetery
not a word was said: mime
with real objects—the coffin
carried from the hearse
over the lawn to graveside
with no noise but indrawn breath.
The pallbearers
were from the Clown Society
but in ordinary clothes,
their sombre faces
free of makeup.

Yet after the casket was lowered
from the chrome frame around the
hole in the earth
and everyone started to leave
except the man with the backhoe

the box bobbed up again.

A member of the burial party
tugged the jacket of the person nearest her
and gestured. This person, too,
alerted others, until all
had reassembled around the coffin
rocking slightly at the surface
over empty air.

A flustered cemetery official
reattached the straps around the casket
and pushed on it.
Once more the wooden box descended
into the ground.
But as soon as the straps were released
the coffin slowly rose

as though the vacant grave
was filling with water
—a ship lifted in a lock.

The third time
the coffin was lowered
the official and two of the clowns
rode it down.
They gathered at one end
while the backhoe
carefully dropped a load of earth
clattering on the lid
and then a second.
The people in the hole
moved to stand awkwardly on the fallen soil

while the backhoe released two more bucketfuls
at the other end.
Then arms reached for the living
and helped them out
as more soil descended.
The casket quivered
        straining against the weight
heaped on it
                forcing down
                        hiding it
away.

When the grave was filled
the ground swelled a little
and the backhoe rolled across the rise
tamping it firm,
level.

No one brought flowers.

CLOWN SEQUENCE: THE MONUMENT TO THE CLOWN

GARISH, people said
of the grave marker

    erected in accordance
    with her request

    scribbled in her diaries
    her nieces found

A conical hat
of concrete
five feet high

    angled jauntily
    topped with a large quartz ball

        the whole painted yellow
        with red stripes

        and wired
        —a small endowment
        meeting the electrical bills

           so neon tubing
           in blue

           crackles in a spiral up the stone
           pulsing on and off at random

           and a tapeloop

           emits nonsense syllables
           amid clacks, beeps, water flushing
           kazoos, car-alarm sirens

WE BURIED MY SON SO HE COULD REST IN PEACE
one letter to the editor complained
WHO GAVE PERMISSION
FOR SUCH A DEVICE
TO DISTURB THE SACRED SLEEP OF THE DEAD
Another letter told how the writer
broke into tears when she visited her parents' plot
at Christmas, after travelling two thousand
kilometers, and found
THIS ABOMINATION
WHY SHOULD ANYONE BE ALLOWED
TO MAKE NOISE IN THIS SETTING
LET ALONE DISTRACT MOURNERS
BY FLASHING LIGHTS
Somebody else in print
likened the monument
to the time the cemetery was overrun
with the burrows of ground squirrels
that eventually had to be poisoned
OUR FAMILY CANNOT MOVE OUR DEAD
WITHOUT GREAT EXPENSE
BUT WE WILL IF THIS PROBLEM
IS NOT DEALT WITH

> For those who approach
> the chattering, blinking
> abandoned stone
>
> the inscription reads
> *O Citizen*
> *Part Of You*
> *Is Buried Here*

THE HALLOWS

A road in the moonlight
and the roses are trembling

What passes down the lane
crosses the dark shadows of trees

toward a house, where leaves are piled on soil
in which tulip bulbs are buried

amid ground-up bones
soaked with water

which will be preserved as liquid
in the frozen earth all winter

What touches the road
is neither wheel nor foot

nor hoof
nor the moon

nor the roses by the gate
trembling

THE ALTS VISIT

They entered my head
as if they walked into another room of
their apartment
by the East River.
They brought their habitual
low-key bickering:
"We want to inform you, concerning Sara,"
Herschel said, "just so you know,
so you understand..."
"Herschel, we agreed
I'm to tell him," Edith cut Herschel off:
"Whenever your mother, whenever Sara
crosses over, we'll meet her.
She won't be alone.
Herschel and I..."
"We'll be there," Herschel interrupted,
"She'll be all right
with us." And then the speech mannerism
that helped define him while he was alive:
"Do you get the, uh...? Do you get the, uh...?"
"Herschel," Edith protested,
"let me finish:
someone is always present
to help when you cross," Edith said.
"Unless," she added, looking
above her half-glasses,
"a person feels he needs to
do this alone, experience this
by himself."
In the sudden silence, I knew Edith spoke
to the tension between
my fears of death and my fears of being
obligated to others.
"But we will meet Sara," Edith continued after a moment.
"Yes, we will," Herschel echoed
out of the dark.

AUTUMN'S GATE

By afternoon, the road
began to enter an autumn country.
Ferns along the shoulder
blurred into brown
as yellow birch leaves
stirred
or floated
above the asphalt.

And I saw in a smoke or mist
that drifted on the hills
the doorway
through which eons of green Aprils,
white Decembers
have passed.

So much has crossed over
what is left to comfort
us who still gather
about autumn's gate?
I believe death may be more filled with
a joyful music
than this side retains.
I think of Blake greeting his death
with happy tunes
—what did he comprehend
of where he was to travel?

In nature's house are many mansions
a wise man said.
If death does not sweep us utterly away
what light streams
from those dwellings?

Are the dead like us who remain
—swung with the planet's turning

into a customary, complicated dark?
Or are the dead a faded smoke
from autumn's fires?

The highway climbs through a mottled wood
of orange larch and green fir.
I do not know if the dead
are lost
or found

or are themselves a road across these valleys
and ridges,
this season.

I'LL BE RIGHT BACK

When the last of my chairs
is loaded on the truck
I'll be right back

The boxes of books
wholesaled away, my files
and trunk full of mementos from childhood
bagged for the trash
I'll be right back

The last poem of mine
finally excised in the anthology revision
I'll be right back

When no one alive
remembers there was a person with my name
I'll be right back

And I don't mean reincarnation
And I don't mean
soul
I don't mean
we're all part of the biosphere
Nor do I mean
random evolutionary chance

I mean I'll be
right back

NOTES

p. 14: "Asphalt Hours, Asphalt Air"—the Rand Formula, named after a decision by Canadian Supreme Court Justice Ivan Rand, was a strike-ending compromise. Under its provisions, employers deduct union dues for all employees whether or not they choose to be union members.

p. 27: "Surprises," along with the following three poems ("Two Students Looking at a Postcard, etc.," "New and Used" and "The Freighter") are set in Vancouver, B.C.

p. 59: "Breath: For Fred Wah" celebrates the Canadian poet Fred Wah (b. 1939) whose work is often situated in the landscapes surrounding Kootenay Lake in southeastern B.C. One of Wah's artistic concerns has been the breath and its influence on poetic form and function.

p. 70: "A Cursing Poem" derives from the cursing poems in Jerome Rothenberg's anthology of aboriginal poetries, *Technicians of the Sacred*. Gordon Shrum was an outspoken B.C. civil servant, who in 1971 when the poem was written was head of the province's electric utility, which also ran the Vancouver municipal transit system. In 1971 the minimum wage was $2 an hour and a bus ride was 25 cents. (As a comparison, when the book from which the poem is taken was published in 1989, the minimum wage had increased two-and-a-quarter times, but it cost five times the 1971 fare to ride the bus.) The reference to "the French" refers to civil unrest in Quebec in 1971, culminating in the federal government's invocation of the War Measures Act suspending civil rights in the whole country.

Shrum once drank a beaker of defoliant at a press conference to convince the public that environmental concerns were not to be taken seriously. The effectiveness of my poem may be gauged by noting that Shrum lived another 14 years after the poem was written.

p. 72: "Marshall-Wells Illumination"—Marshall-Wells was the name of a former chain of wholesale-retail hardware stores in Western Canada.

pp. 75, 79: "The Poet Milton Acorn Crosses into the Republic of Heaven" and "In a Small House on the Outskirts of Heaven" refer to Milton Acorn (1923–1986), a Canadian poet from Prince Edward Island known for his writing on social themes.

p. 93: "A Yellow Cottage" is in memory of Joan Partridge Crocker.

p. 141: "Waley, Waley"—the title is from an alternate chorus (and alternate title) to the folk song usually known as "The Water Is Wide."